ZINGA ZINGA ZA!

ZINGA ZINGA ZA!

John Fischetti

Follett Publishing Company

Chicago

Library of Congress Catalog Card Number: 73-85002
ISBN: 0–695–80422–7
First printing

For Karen, Peter and Michael

A little over a year ago, Ron Dorfman, Editor of the *Chicago Journalism Review,* introduced me to Patricia Meehan, the Senior Editor of Follett Publishing Company. I want to thank Ron for setting off a chain of events that resulted finally in the realization of a life-long desire to have a book of my cartoons printed.

It's impossible to thank Pat Meehan enough for leading and guiding me through the terribly unfamiliar thicket of words. My business is pictures and I needed a lot of help with the words. Pat, young, bright, and patient, was right there where I needed her—all the time.

I asked Peter Lisagor, my old friend and former Editor when we were both on *Stars and Stripes,* to write the Introduction. Pete asked for the manuscript; he asked for a batch of cartoons; he asked for the edited manuscript; old friends of mine phoned that Pete had been questioning them about me. I had had no idea he was going to be that thorough.

I phoned Pete and asked him why he was doing all this—after twenty-eight years didn't he know me? Obviously, after twenty-eight years it was I who didn't know my friend. His actions were the moves of the great journalistic pro he is.

For his confidence in me, I thank Jock Whitney, Publisher of the *New York Herald Tribune,* who gave me my first absolutely free rein as a political cartoonist.

To Kenneth McArdle, who edited my first drafts out of friendship and the goodness of his heart, I owe a great deal.

I'm indebted to Alfredo Siani of Alitalia Airlines, who took the time to teach me the difference between Italian and Neapolitan. He is responsible for correcting and confirming all the Neapolitan words used in the book.

I wrote the whole thing in longhand so I'm very grateful to Marion Denniston of the Editorial Department of the *Chicago Daily News* and to Kari Naglestad of Follett Publishing Company for helping my words take their first steps.

For Pansy Charlotte Weill, who helped me a long time ago, my deep affection.

And finally and always, my loving thanks to Karen on this, our twenty-fifth anniversary year.

CONTENTS

FOREWORD

There are writers who look upon editorial cartoonists as saboteurs of the Word, as sly and inventive characters who doodle for a living. The reason is simple enough: pure envy.

Writers must cope with the treachery of words. They often find ideas as unwieldy as the lifting of a piano with bare hands. Their world is one of caveats, on-the-other-hands, howevers, and other abstract qualifiers. Nevertheless (see what I mean!), they must persuade an increasingly skeptical audience that they will come out somewhere near a demonstrable truth. It's not easy work, especially for those who write politics. In fact, it's a bit like dancing on a sponge, and in terms of wear and tear on the nervous system, it is sometimes cruelly debilitating.

Now enter the cartoonists. Those ungainly little pictures they draw mock the writer. Their work falls somewhere between ancient hieroglyphics and contemporary grafitti, without being as sacred as the first or as profane as the second. With a few deft scratches, a curved line here and a drooping one there, a jowl swollen with greed or an eye leaking malice, they somehow manage to say funny and profound things. Imprisoned in their squares and rectangles is a good deal of the inhumanity, outrage and avarice of the world around them. Their message is instantly recognizable, and, what's most exasperating to the writing man, they don't bother winding up to deliver it. They come right at you, straight between the eyes, whammo! They are the heavy hitters of journalism. And it all looks so damned easy!

Is it any wonder that writers regard with envy this strange adult breed that still dabbles with crayon?

But as John Fischetti, one of the best of the breed, insists, he didn't "pop full-blown and ink-stained onto this planet." Those scratches and lines started somewhere in the past, took shape and meaning in some urban alley, on a farm, at school, or wherever values are formed for most of us. In Fischetti's case, a large, expressive Italian family full of *linguini*, lousy jokes and love, mainly love, had a lot to do with how his pictures turn out. So did the neighbors in Brooklyn, the guys and gals he met as a part-time Depression hobo and a messboy aboard ships, the fakers, the hustlers, the teachers and fellow artists he met at Pratt who inspired him. In Fischetti's case, the earth and the sky also played a role.

When I first met Fischetti in Paris, during World War II, I expected that a GI with that name, out of Brooklyn and the Great Depression, a knockabout, to be tough, jaded, sour, unhappy. He had to be an unmeltable ethnic. This was long before social and political scientists discovered that ethnics were people with a consciousness of their own, long before those proud buttons, "Kiss me, I'm Italian," had been invented. If Fischetti had devised a button of ethnic awareness in those days, it would have been likely to read, "I'm Italian, and if you don't like it, how about a belt in the mouth?" Or so I thought.

Then I saw his watercolors. Delicate pastel scenes of the Brittany coast, warm, gentle, sensitive. The stereotype fled, and there stood a guy with deep currents of gentleness and, if you would believe it, innocence. In time, it became apparent that a small Vesuvius also bubbled just below the surface. But it was a kind of naive wonderment about everything that crossed his bow that impressed his GI comrades. We shared an apartment with others in Porte du St. Cloud and moonlighted together on the *Paris Post*, a civilian newspaper, for a brief time. In a nominal way, he worked for me when I was editor of a *Stars & Stripes* magazine. Everybody else on the magazine understood that I was busy with other matters and took their grievances and psychic urges and ambitious projects to an assistant who really ran the supplement. But not Fischetti. I had to conjure up special assignments for him, talk them over with him, bounce ideas back and forth—in return for which he laughed at my dismal jokes. I think in retrospect I got the better of the exchange.

Fischetti was then, as now, radiant with a *joie de vivre*, an unaccountable zest, or as he puts it, "an insatiable appetite for people and places." And we became drinking buddies, after a fashion. Neither of us belted the cognac much, but we did get an uproarious lift from a French fruit drink, a *poupée*. In Paris in the summer and fall of 1945, that was the only stimulant needed.

It was quite clear then that Fischetti would be what he became. Even then he was cataloguing his frustrations and indignation over the remediable wickedness he encountered. He was intensely earnest about the issues of his time, and he was already well on the way toward developing what Bruce Biossat, another old journalistic crony, calls "a unity of attitude" about such verities as justice, freedom, individual dignity. The yahoos who mistake dissent for destructiveness, who see a subversive in every protester, would probably reject the notion that Fischetti is, at bottom, a conservative, a "square" who believes in the immigrant ethic of his beloved blonde mother, which embraces hard work, hard study, parental respect, a belief in God, a fair shake for every human being. But it is true, of course, as is his burnished sense of outrage in the face of false pieties, deceitfulness, and injustice.

Fischetti knew what it was to be bullied in Brooklyn, and he learned how to deal with bullies. He did it with broomsticks as a kid; he used a pen when he grew up. As he describes the sweaty, mystical process of creating cartoons, he rummages about in the news for ideas, prodded by the prosaic notion that "a cartoonist's ass is on the line." But, in truth, where he really finds his ideas is less in the news than in himself, in a concern for the simple verities. The essence of a Fischetti cartoon is more than a visual experience. It's really a cram course in the human condition, as you shall see.

    Peter Lisagor

PREFACE

Whatever I am as a cartoonist, a political cartoonist, has been determined by the many people who have inspired me. All my life I've wanted to do something for the poor and the unfortunate whom I was surrounded with when I was young. The schemers, the opportunists, and the vested interests I never gave a damn about. They take care of their own interests quite well.

Inspiration came from my family, my classmates, my church, and all the great journalists.

In my particular field, there are Nast, Minor, Young, Rollin Kirby, Herblock, Mauldin, Fitzpatrick, Low, Vicky, Conrad, Oliphant.

There are the two comic strip cartoonists who were giants during the McCarthy nightmare, Walt Kelly and Al Capp, who were great political cartoonists during the darkness, when even powerful political men were timid.

I've tried to use what talent I have to do my damnedest to make things just a little better, to alleviate some suffering and neaten up this spaceship we all live on for such a short time. My greatest wish would be that some young man or woman will find something good in my life and try to emulate whatever it is. Hopefully, they'll find something in my political cartooning, but I'll settle for any progress in any other field.

xiii

ZINGA ZINGA ZA!

When I was growing up, I had a goofy cousin who lived on a farm in Rahway, New Jersey. His answer to any question, no matter what, was "Zinga Zinga Za!"

"Did you wash your face?"

"Zinga Zinga Za!"

"Where's your old man?"

"Zinga Zinga Za!"

"You goofy or somethin'?"

"Zinga Zinga Za!"

His replies made about as much sense as a lot of the answers we get from the politicians and the military today who seem to be guiding us down the road to oblivion. Like my goofy cousin they are responsible for Zinga Zinga Zas like:

"We had to destroy the town to save it."
An American Colonel in Vietnam

"The statement that we are in a complete stalemate is complete fiction. It is completely unrealistic. During the past year tremendous progress has been made."
General William C. Westmoreland
Vietnam, 1966

"The President is aware of what is going on in Southeast Asia. That is not to say anything is going on in Southeast Asia."

February 1971, when Ron Ziegler, Presidential Press Secretary, was asked whether a Laotian incursion was planned.

"We must halt the erosion of moral fiber in American life and the denial of individual accountability for individual action."

Richard M. Nixon, during the 1972 presidential campaign, otherwise known as the era of the Watergate scandal.

"There are a lot of mediocre judges and people and lawyers. They are entitled to a little representation, aren't they?"

Senator Roman Hruska (R.-Neb.), in support of the nomination of Judge G. Harrold Carswell to the U.S. Supreme Court

"Why was the U.S.S. *Liberty* stationed so close to the fighting that Israeli planes and torpedo boats attacked it, killing thirty-four American sailors?"

"—the position (of the ship) was required so that the U.S.S. *Liberty* could use the moon as a passive reflector for its communications."

Pentagon

For me, the point of political cartooning is to try to take some of the Zing out of the Zinga Zinga Zas! Years ago, I thought, or rather, I *knew* I could do it. But today, I often have an uneasy feeling that I'm going down for the third time between Zinga Zinga and Za!

However that may be, this book attempts to shed some light on the strange breed that political cartoonists are. Since there are only about 250 political cartoonists in this country, the average citizen seldom runs into one.

In fact, I once ran into a man who had the idea that there was only one. I was getting my shoes shined in a Greyhound Bus Terminal on 34th Street in New York City some years ago. The shoeshine man noticed that a worn crease on the outside of my shoe was resisting his best efforts to put a shine on it. He asked me how it got there. I replied that I was a cartoonist and always rested my foot sideways on the base of my drawing board while working.

At the mention of the word "cartoonist," his eyes lighted up and he asked what comic strip I drew. I told him I didn't draw a comic strip, I drew political cartoons. His eyes lit up even brighter than before, and he asked incredulously, "*You* the man who draw all those donkeys and elephants?!!"

And even after all these years I still find people who react with total noncomprehension when they find out I'm a cartoonist. I hasten to assure them that I did not pop full blown and ink stained onto this planet, but was born like any other normal earthling, weighing about sixteen pounds.

LITTLE ITALY

On September 27, 1916, at 55 DeKalb Avenue, I, Giovanni Fischetti, was born, the *bambino* or baby of a large family in the Navy Yard section of Brooklyn. My first impressions were of furious hand signals, heady smells of *linguini* and *paste fasule,* and general bedlam. It was an Italian family.

"Little Italy" in Brooklyn was always crowded with pushcarts and people. The decibel level was very high. The people were warm and loving. At the first sign of spring life was lived mostly on the street, shopping, gossiping, stealing from push-carts, singing "*Ue Mari*" from a stoop, playing the numbers.

Then one day I heard, "Ged owda here, you little Dago sunavabitch," and I realized that there were Unfriendlies in the world with me. Obviously, some people had not been born into the world of *linguini, paste fasule* and the same hand signals I found so comforting.

The neighborhood was supposed to be tough but I don't remember it that way. There were so damned many people who loved you. Your family, your relatives and friends. You saw them protecting each other against the outside forces and you felt safe there.

In the early days we were surrounded with neighbors who were struggling to survive and some kids had parents who copped out because the load was too heavy. These kids hit the streets and did what they could to survive. Some shined shoes, some sold newspapers, others started getting into trouble with the law.

But I came from a family that was hacking it. We had love, warmth and very happy times. In fact, the very size of the family, with all the relatives and close friends, gave us a sense of indomitability. Yet we were very much aware of being an island in this country, and so we clung together like Pilgrims.

Emanuela or Minnie or Min or Mom or Mama mia had come to the United States at the age of sixteen from the village of Siano in the Province of Salerno in Italy.

She was a strawberry blonde with blue eyes and a fair complexion. Because her husband and all of her children had black hair and deep brown eyes, this made her doubly special to us—she was Mom and she was a blonde Italian. Not many Southern Italians are, and almost all the Italians I was raised with were from the south of Italy. They were mostly Neapolitans, and some were from Calabria or Sicilia.

When Emanuela arrived in America, her family settled in a tenement on the Lower East Side of New York City, smack in the middle of Little Italy, right next to China Town.

Mom went to work immediately in a sweat shop, basting, and sewing buttons on coats. Two years after arriving here she married young Pietro Fischetti.

By the time we knew him, Pietro or Pete, my father, was a stout man about five feet seven inches tall, and his hair was black. It was just a fringe, about an inch and a half wide, which girdled half his skull. The rest of his head was bare, smooth, and glistened magnificently.

His ablutions every morning were something to behold. He'd lean over, palms outstretched, and form a cup with his hands. Then he'd catch the water from the tap, and raising his waterfilled hands to his face, he would exhale and make a noise not unlike a horse neighing. Repeatedly, he would crash the water over his face and skull. Then he'd towel his face and head vigorously and that was that.

I was absolutely fascinated and longed for the day when I would be bald like my father and not have to contend with a tangled mass of hair every morning.

Ironically, my nearly bald father was a barber with a shop on DeKalb Avenue and Flatbush Avenue Extension. He also moonlighted as a barber at Brooklyn Hospital on nights and weekends. He carried a satchel containing hair clippers, scissors, combs, brushes, bottles of perfumed hair tonic, straight razors, shaving mugs and talcum powder. It weighed a ton. He would go from bed to bed performing his chores on the patients and he also barbered the young interns and some doctors.

He also played the hell out of a lot of musical instruments. But his main love, and ours, was the mandolin. With it, Pete brightened up any room he walked into. People radiated when he started playing. It apparently filled the older people with nostalgic thoughts of the Old Country. Why these thoughts should have made them happy always eluded me, since all I had ever heard about Naples were stories of grinding poverty and hunger, and frightening stories of earthquakes.

Some of the young interns at Brooklyn Hospital were also amateur musicians, and along with Pete, they were paid to play some gigs at weddings and parties. I don't know if they played any Bar Mitzvahs.

The first thing Pete always did when he arrived home every night was to take off his heavy, black, high-topped shoes with their metal arch supports. He would then roll up the bottoms of his trousers and put his feet, covered with formidable-looking corns and bunions, into a pan of hot water. His ecstatic expression and his sigh of relief were signals in our home that all was right with the world. A gregarious man, he enjoyed his work. It was hell on the feet, but his contact with people afforded him great pleasure.

Pete and Minnie's first child lived only eighteen months. Then Guiseppe or Joe, my oldest living brother, arrived. A miscarriage of twins followed. Later, Anna, Jeanne, Henry and I. We were all delivered by midwives.

My brother Joe is eleven years older than I. The earliest memories I have of him are when he was already about eighteen or nineteen. He was tall and very thin, and like all the young men of that era, he emulated the style of Rudolph Valentino, with his patent leather hair slicked back, long sideburns and unsmiling mien. Trousers were worn tight at the knee and bell-bottomed.

I remember Joe leaving the Sunday dinner table. He would look at Dad, rub his index finger and thumb together and say, "Hey, Pop, see me go?!!" It was his way of asking for spending money.

Joe started driving trucks and has driven them all his life. When I was about twelve, he would take me with him on Saturdays as he picked up loads in Brooklyn and ran them over to the docks in New York City. Joe had tattoos on his big muscular arms. I would watch him in wide-eyed wonder, while he wrestled the pre-power steering wheel, bulling the truck through the packed city streets, cursing at everybody in his way.

I only run into Joe at family funerals now—Funny, it used to be funerals and weddings.

My sister Jeanne is five years older than I am. She was always a very attractive young woman who drew appreciative glances from men, young and old. She went to Hefley's Business School after high school and after that went to work in the administration office of Brooklyn Hospital where Dad moonlighted. She married Charlie Zambri and had three children, one of whom died.

Then there's Anna, the oldest girl, who's nine years older than I. She was the surrogate mother to all of us except Joe. She was always in charge of Henry and me when Mom was away working in my grandmother's grocery store.

She still tells the story of her fat-faced, brown-eyed baby brother's first solo in the world. When I was two and Henry was four, she and Jeanne took Henry and me to Fort Greene Park, which is bounded on three sides by streets. The fourth side is bounded by Brooklyn Hospital and, at the farthest end, by the Raymond Street Jail. Everyone was having a good time, and Anna and Jeanne grew careless about watching me. I disappeared, and they searched for me frantically, everywhere.

At last, at the farthest tip of the park, they saw the fat ass of their fat baby brother, casually strolling along, hands clasped behind his back. I was rescued, and my adventures were more carefully supervised after that.

Anna is also the one who introduced our family to American food. Every Saturday afternoon was American food time: she always cooked French fried potatoes, and from week to week, she alternated between hamburgers, hot dogs and every great so often, steak.

Henry and I loved American Saturday afternoons, although Saturday nights were another thing entirely. Then Anna and Jeanne gave Henry and me baths. That part of Saturday we could have done without.

Most families are pretty lucky—they have one mother. We were twice blessed—we had Anna, too.

Although I still see both my sisters and their children from time to time, it's certainly not as often since we moved to Chicago.

Mom was the epitome of the immigrant ethic, always thinking about work, learning, and bettering the family's lot. She had had about the equivalent of a third-grade education in Italy and all of her life she considered school the number one priority for her children. Whenever my brother or I indicated a desire to quit school, she would quickly put an end to that kind of thinking by telling us sternly that we were going to school until we tripped over our beards.

Mom's idea of Nirvana was for her boys to grow up and go to a job wearing a shirt and tie. She never let up on education because to her it was the escape hatch from a life of pushcarts, picks and shovels, and poverty. In her wildest dreams, she had the shirt and tie on a doctor or lawyer son.

I had a mild coronary in the middle of doing this book. It occurred to me while lying in bed in the hospital that Mom's hopes for me of Success in America had succeeded far beyond her wildest dreams. I was not just going to work in a clean shirt and wearing a tie, but lying down, not with just a little success symbol like an ulcer, but living it up with an executive-type heart attack! All the way! Top of the world, Ma!

Within the confines of our home, Mom was a great mimic and actress and she often regaled us with imitations of the people we knew. Anyone who came into the house was fair game for her mimicry, male or female, neighbor or stranger.

One of her specialties was a little guy who looked like Mr. Punch. He was toothless, and his hooked nose and pointed chin almost touched when he wasn't talking. In addition, he was always mooching food, a belt of booze or worn clothing from Grandma or the neighbors. Everyone called him The Millionaire, and Mom had everything about him down cold, from his toothlessness to his posture and the very timbre of his whine. It was like having your own stand-up comic in the family.

She was the hub of what must have been the kissingest family ever. Mom kissed Pop, the kids kissed Mom and Pop, the relatives kissed the kids. When I was sent down to the cellar to get a bottle of the wine that Dad had made, everybody at the dinner table kissed me good-bye and then kissed me hello when I returned, two minutes later. I greeted my Dad with a kiss right up to the time he died and by then I was forty-two years old and the father of two sons.

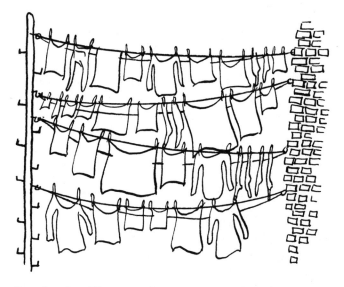

Day to day life was always very noisy. The rooms echoed with arguments, laughter, crying, music. Hand gestures and histrionics helped to keep the air circulating.

Something was always going on the stove. Coffee, certainly, simmering sauce or *suchillo*, or beans soaking in a pot. I'd watch, fascinated, while Mom rolled dough, cut big pieces off the large mound and then expertly chopped them into little one-inch pieces. She'd then put her thumb in the center, apply some pressure and roll the dough out flat into about two inch circles, to make a *cavatilla-*

—a little hat. These were boiled in water, drained, and then covered with some succulent meat sauce.

Buciarde was a dirty word to my mother. It meant liar, and it was anathema to her. You would never run out of moral credit with Mom if you levelled with her.

So even if it was a punishable offense, and you *knew* you'd be punished if you told the truth, you told the truth. You were not rewarded by not being punished. Punishment usually began with the sentence, "*Piglia a fune,*" which meant, "Go get the two-foot piece of garden hose."

It may seem unlikely that a kid would have to fetch the piece of garden hose he'd be whacked across the ass with, but Mom ran a tight ship and it never occurred to us to debate the issue.

When Dad was around and my brother and I were unruly, she'd look his way and call to him. He'd glare in our direction and yell, "*Mannaggia!*" or "Damn!" When he started unloosening his belt, we'd dive out the door. Unloosening his belt was as far as Dad ever went: I never remember his laying a glove on us, but it was a great act.

During the week breakfast consisted of coffee and *vascuotte,* which was a chunk of dry whole wheat bread, about three by four inches. You could dip it in coffee to soften it, or just bite into the dry stuff. I suppose our excellent teeth may be partly

attributed to that daily practice.

Sunday breakfast was really looked forward to. Every Sunday morning Mom would pour the coffee, to which she and only she would add the milk which was in such scarce supply in our house. With the coffee, we had slices from a large round Italian loaf of white bread with a wonderful crispy crust. Dad would put the loaf up against his chest and pull the knife toward his throat, cutting away. He wasn't unique in this: all the men and women in the neighborhood cut bread this way. Dad then spread tub butter on the slices of bread and handed them around to the salivating family.

After breakfast and cleaning up we'd head toward the Italian Presbyterian Church, our church. How we ever got there was a tribute to my father. He was quite a man in a way that I didn't fully appreciate until I was much older and learned a lot more about people and the difficulties of the world.

We lived, of course, in Little Italy and all of our friends and relatives were Catholics. When I was six, my father decided that Catholicism was not the answer to what he was looking for. He shopped around from church to church each Sunday for many months, with the family in tow. In the end, we became Italian Presbyterians. He was surrounded by Catholics and I don't imagine they took kindly to this. I never heard that he was ostracized for doing this, but that may have been due as much to his being a very tough man as that he was a very gentle, pleasant human being.

Then one Sunday, when I was about nine, my mother had a confrontation with the minister of the church. My brother and I were accused of breaking a lock on a cabinet and stealing some hymn books. Mom was incensed. She looked at us and asked if we were guilty of this offense. We said no. As I pointed out before, we never lied to Mom and she knew it. She then asked if we knew who had done it and we answered yes. She didn't pursue this since she wasn't interested in who had done it, just so it wasn't her boys. My mother looked at the minister and said her family would never come to this church again.

My Mom stood eyeball to eyeball with an Italian Presbyterian minister. He blinked and I wound up a German Lutheran.

After Mom stormed out of that church we went home to Bedford Avenue. It was in the Bedford-Stuyvesant section of Brooklyn, for by then we had moved uptown from the Navy Yard. Mom never stopped moving us further uptown, away from Navy Street, where she was sure disaster lurked for the family.

Back home, she told my brother and me to walk to St. Peter's German Lutheran Church, about a block away, and ask the minister if we could join his congregation. Right now. Same day.

Dutifully, we walked over and asked the pastor if we could join. He had a marvelous face, silver hair, a mustache, a goatee, gentle eyes and a ruddy complexion. It seemed we were welcome.

The congregation consisted of German immigrants and their first-generation American children. Later on, when we joined the Boy Scout troop in this church, it was always strange to hear the roll call: "Doscher, Deutschmann, Douker, Fischetti, H., Fischetti, J., Grosser, Gunther . . ." In school even more than in the German Lutheran Church, I found out that everyone was not a member of a large Italian family.

While it may have read "Giovanni" on the birth certificate, as soon as we denizens of Little Italy hit the American public school system, the Anglo-Saxon teachers changed us Giovannis, Guiseppes, and Enricos to Johnny, Joe, and Henry. So I became John or Johnny, and it stayed with me for the rest of my life, except among family members and relatives. But it got worse than that.

The neighborhood I was raised in was divided into three parts, Italian, Irish and black. Our mortal enemies were the Irish since they were right next to us, and were between us and the blacks. We had enough trouble with the Irish, so we never went

11

cross town to beg more trouble from the blacks. At school, we all mixed socially, usually with sticks, rocks and fists.

In the whole school there was one Jew. The Italians ran with the Italians, the Irish with the Irish, the blacks with the blacks. The Jewish boy just ran. Going to or coming from school, one cluster or another of blacks, Irish or Italians were always in hot pursuit, ready to beat him up. I'm afraid I was in the ranks of the pursuers on many occasions. I don't remember anyone catching the Jewish kid, much less his ever being beaten. But to this day I have qualms of conscience thinking of the terrible fear-filled days that boy endured, some of them at my hand.

Then we transferred to Mark Hopkins Junior High School, which was about three times further away than the school we had attended before, and in the opposite direction. It was smack in the middle of an impoverished Jewish ghetto, and the student population at Hopkins was about 99% Jewish. I found that unlike the Christians at my former school, the Jews didn't curse at and chase Christians, simply because we were different and they outnumbered us.

So, taking for granted that Jews always ran when threatened, on one of my first days at Hopkins, I walked up to a boy and pushed and cursed at him.

It was just to establish how things were going to be now, with this influx of *goyim*. However, he not only didn't run, he pushed back. Then he knocked me from one end of the school yard to the other. My first thought after pulling myself together was how decent it had been of that Jewish kid at my other school to outrun me all the time.

But being Italian by no means precluded trouble with fellow Italians. At school one day a *paisane* or countryman of mine took umbrage at a sneering remark of mine and laid one on my lip.

My brother Henry, watching me wash the blood away at the six-faucet drinking trough, demanded to know who had done it. He found out and proceeded to pound hell out of our fellow Italian.

I was sent to the office of our WASP principal, a woman who looked like an angry eagle. A bloody handkerchief covered my tattered lip, and my attacker came along, fresh from my brother's lumping. The principal asked me to remove the handkerchief, then shrieked when I uncovered my lip. She then proceeded to beat the piss out of my attacker. My wound started to look superficial, compared to the knots my adversary was accumulating.

I was sent to the Brooklyn Hospital Emergency Clinic to get stitched. My tooth had gone through my upper lip and it took a couple of stitches to set my sneer straight again.

When I arrived home, my mother shrieked and wanted to go after my assailant. Only after she was informed that a member of our family had had vengeance did Mom simmer down.

At the end of every school year my brother and I had all our hair cut off. Dad didn't want to bother cutting our hair at intervals during the summer, so he simply cut it all off then. Our denuded skulls made excellent targets for the older boys and it was great sport for them to make bombing runs at our gourds. It stung like hell and one older, larger boy in particular delighted in stinging us.

One day Mom found me crying in the area way of our brownstone on Bedford Avenue. My brother and I were both holding our stinging bald heads. Alarmed, she asked us what happened. When we told her, she wanted to know why we had allowed the boys to hit us. We told her this particular boy was much bigger than us, but she replied that *no* one was bigger than us. We were puzzled until she clarified things: *"Piglia a mazze"*—get a stick or a club. She was of course talking about an equalizer.

Next day we had two broomsticks in the area way. Henry gripped one firmly and put the other against the wall nearby. I was sent out as bait to lure our tormentor into the area way. The lout's lust for my glistening dome was all that occupied his thoughts, and he chased me furiously. I came flying into the area way, with the larger boy not far behind. As he rounded the corner, Henry swung and belted him right on the forehead. He went to his knees. I grabbed my broomstick and started to pound away in between my brother's shots.

Covering his head, stumbling, our former tormentor managed a successful retreat. From that day on he used to nod and say, "Hello, Henry," "Hello, Johnny," whenever he saw us. He must have passed the word because we weren't bothered that way again. Mom was quite a good teacher about the lessons of life.

Then there was my grandmother, Josie Vivo, called Nonnona, who cracked walnuts with her teeth even when she was in her seventies. I have to marvel now, looking back at Nonnona's life on Navy Street. Here was a sturdy little Italian widow who always wore an apron with change always clinking in the right-hand pocket. But she was a real entrepreneur—she put every inch of the two-story frame house in which she lived to use.

On the ground floor was the tiny grocery store. Behind the store was the little dining room where we ate through the interruptions of skid row types coming in to buy a belt of Nonnona's bootleg booze. A pint bottle was always kept on the middle divider of an orange crate standing on its side in

the dining room. Then behind the dining room was another tiny room with the stove on which dinner was cooked.

The production part of the booze operation was on the second floor. When I was about eight and my brother Henry was ten, we used to go upstairs to help pour the alcohol out of the tins of alcohol purchased from the local bootlegger. We funneled it into pint and half-pint whiskey bottles and then stuck labels on the bottles. The guys who came in to buy in the dining room below could either get individual shots or purchase the bottles.

Nonnona was busted a few times. It happened sometimes, when the wires got crossed and some cop hadn't been paid off. All the little shopkeepers with operations going paid off.

Once during a bust, my brother Henry hurled himself at a bull whose shoes were bigger than Henry was. The detective flicked him off like a gnat. Henry caromed off the opposite wall.

And then the cops carted Granny off to the station house. Everybody in the neighborhood ran around digging up enough bail money to spring her. They always did, whenever anyone was busted.

But the boozery was not the only attraction of Nonnona's house. There were two other rooms on the second floor. Directly over the dining room was a storage room of no special interest, but next to that, over the store, was Nonnona's bedroom. It always reeked of wintergreen and Sloan's Linament, and although I never did actual!y see her use it, I guess she had it to soothe her old bones.

On the bureau and in every corner of Nonnona's room was all sorts of junk, of the kind that would delight any young boy. Inexplicably, she had a fencing foil and a fencer's mask. There were hats and little ceramic figures, and all kinds of shoes, some of them without mates. I don't know why she collected all this stuff or where she got it, but she always had it. It was one of the few places in the house that didn't seem to be there to turn over an extra buck.

Besides selling the groceries and candy and peddling the booze, she had another little operation. Downstairs, to the left of the grocery store, was a cobblestone passageway that led to a stable in the rear of the house. Nonnona rented space both to the peddlers with pushcarts who parked them there at the end of the day, and to four or five peddlers with horses and wagons who bedded their horses in the stable and parked their wagons up against the wall of the six-story tenement that rose up next to Nonnona's house.

There was a water trough with a faucet right outside the alley window in the dining room of Nonnona's house. The peddlers, after unhitching their horses from the wagons, walked them over to the trough—within inches of the window where my brother and I always stood. We'd watch the horses take great gulps of water, and gaze, fascinated, as an area around each horse's temple would recess and then fill out, recess and fill out. The horses' heads seemed enormous.

I loved going to my grandmother's grocery store. Besides the fun we always had there, life just teemed in the street outside. The great St. Vincent's Day feast was celebrated on Navy Street once a year and then joy reigned everywhere for many, many days.

For about three or four blocks, the streets were festooned with lights, and pushcarts and vending stalls were set up bumper to bumper the whole length. The street was closed to traffic and the people milled about on the sidewalks and in the middle of the street. The peddlers sold miniature buggy whips, clams, hats and paper cups of shaved ice with multi-colored sweet juices squirted all over.

At the stalls, they sold strings of little round filbert nuts all hung together like a necklace. There was *dorrone*, a hard candy with almonds in it, and hero sandwiches of peppers, onions, and sausages in between two heroic pieces of Italian bread. There were pizzas, beer, soda pop, roasted chestnuts and ice cream. We ran up and down the street, in and out between the pushcarts and stalls, eating, laughing, singing.

A band on a specially constructed stand played arias from various operas. The notes of trumpet solos reverberated up and down the gaily lit, crowded blocks full of Italians enjoying themselves.

15

On the last day of the feast, all of the Catholic Church dignitaries marched down the street behind men carrying a banner painted with a likeness of St. Vincent. People stepped out of the crowds and pinned money on the banner. I remember looking goggle-eyed at all those dollar bills pinned to the banner. Then everyone marched to church, where services for St. Vincent were held.

Finally of course the lights came down, the stalls and the bandstand were dismantled, and the accumulated debris was swept away by the street cleaners. The cleaners were called White Wings in the newspapers because of their big, ill-fitting, white uniforms. They each pushed a little wheeled stand containing a big ashcan and they carried large brooms and shovels. After a feast or parade in Brooklyn, they were usually out in force.

The White Wings emptied their cans of debris into a larger two-wheeled horse-drawn conveyance. Especially after some of the large military parades, there were lots of horse apples all over the streets. I remember the sparrows feasting on them before the White Wings scooped them up.

Then near the corner of Myrtle Avenue was Piro's Funeral Home, where life stopped teeming. They were always carting people out in coffins. The horse-drawn funeral wagons had glass sides so everyone could see the casket inside.

The horses had netting all over their heads, necks, backs, and rumps. About half-way down their legs the netting ended and tassles dangled every two or three inches.

Almost all adult funerals had horses in black netting pulling black carriages. White netting and carriage were used when the carriage contained an infant's coffin, or a child who had just been confirmed or was near confirmation when he or she died.

White netting was used for an adult when someone like Graciella, a friend of ours, died in childbirth. She must have died just before the child was born, because her stomach was very large, when she lay in her coffin.

I remember at that wake how everyone was sure her little seven- or eight-year-old son would die of a broken heart because his mother had been taken so early. But he looked pretty vigorous to me days, weeks, even years after the funeral.

The wake and funeral were always experiences in themselves. The bodies would be taken to Piro's Funeral Home for embalming. Then they would be returned to their homes for the wake.

The coffin containing the deceased was placed in a corner of the apartment he formerly lived in. Flowers sent by the family and friends were placed around the coffin. Long candles provided the only light in the room.

One or two rooms were cleared of furniture and camp chairs rented from the funeral home were placed around the room.

Chairs placed near the head and foot of the coffin were occupied by the immediate family. On the outside door or to the side of the door was a crepe, fashioned of flowers and some thin gauze material, notifying all that death was a visitor in this house.

The women in the family, wearing black, spoke softly to each other. The men of the family stood either at the door, greeting friends and relatives come to pay their last respects to the deceased, or in a back room having a glass of wine and talking about incidents in the life of the dear departed.

The visitors offered their condolences to the men at the door and then to the women of the family.

After the weepy offering of regrets, the visitors kneeled, crossed themselves, prayed awhile. They then stood up, looked mournfully at the deceased, wax-like and rouged, and moved on to empty camp chairs. By this time the dead one's family would have simmered down, only to rise to another high decibel of mourning accompanied by new tears and more hand-wringing when the front door opened up again and more friends or relatives arrived.

This would go on for a couple of days until, on the third day, the priest said the final words before the top of the casket was brought down and the loved one became forever a shadow.

The horse-drawn carriages always had funeral bands marching behind them. The walking musicians played long, drawn-out mournful dirges. As the funeral procession went by, strangers crossed themselves, men doffed their hats, and everyone looked as sad as possible. When the carriage contained a tiny, white casket the mournful looks were not labored; they came naturally.

The funeral entourage would make one full turn around the block that the deceased lived on, before the trip to the cemetery.

At the cemetery, as the casket was being lowered into the earth, came the most poignant and tearful scene.

For the most histrionically talented, this was their moment in the sun. I remember many wild passes at throwing oneself into the grave after the casket had been lowered, but the throwee was always restrained by others.

I remember wondering as a kid what it would be like if someone really made it and did go flying down the open grave. It never came to pass, at least not in my crowd.

Across the street from Nonnona's grocery store, the men who played cards and drank coffee in the cafe would stop when a tiny little man, less than five feet tall, would come by. He'd listen to one of the card players who would sit with his chair turned around, his forearms resting on the top of the back of the chair. Then the little man would jot something down on a slip of paper. He was a numbers man.

Everybody played the numbers on Navy Street. You told the numbers guy what numbers you were going for that day, gave him a cent or a few cents, depending on how high a roller you were, and he'd jot your number down next to your initial.

The last few numbers of a Treasury figure that appeared in the paper the next day determined whether you won a few bucks or not.

Sometimes this little guy would come running down the street stuffing the evidence in his mouth, trying to swallow it before a pursuing cop nailed him. Although he didn't always escape, he was a neighbor, so he would be bailed out and back on the street soon after the bust.

There was a settlement house a few blocks away from our house, where we could play games, read, or do whatever to keep us off the streets and out of trouble.

I don't remember spending very much time there but I liked what they called the "outings," and whenever they had one, we'd turn out *en masse.*

One steaming, Brooklyn summer day, we found out they were having an "outing" at the settlement house. We all turned up; we knew it always lasted the entire day, so we carried a couple of sandwiches with us.

They took us to a grassy plot out in a field in New Jersey. There was a big puddle of water with a log floating around in it. The Jersey mosquitoes, as big and nasty as barn bosses, beat the bejesus out of us all afternoon, while we got lobster-red and whooped it up in the puddle.

At the end of the day, they hauled the bitten, burnt lot of us back to the settlement house. We could hardly wait for the next trip to America's Great Outdoors.

Then there were the more routine pleasures. Word got around, as it usually does when there's a great bargain to be found, that there was a movie house—the cheapest around—on Skillman Street and Myrtle Avenue about a mile away from Navy Street. Its formal name was the Skillman. But among us young Italian *cognoscentis* it was simply The Dump.

It was small and smelly, kids just pissed on the floor, and every hour or so a man carrying a vaporizer pumped cheap smelly perfume into the turgid air. I became aware of the smell only when the film's story line bogged down in a love scene.

Candy pushers went up and down the aisles all the time, all day long, day in and day out. The films were silent and the piano player banged away all day. They must have been the only people outside the Pennsylvania coal mine area with black lung.

The first day of *my* dream began when I was in kindergarten, when I was handed a box of colored chalk. I drew an Easter basket, a rabbit and colored eggs. From that day on, I was the artist among my classmates. All through school, I was the guy who could draw.

Mom was always kind of proud of this but to her it wasn't serious. The shirt and tie dream was the important thing. Whenever someone would ask where Johnny was, she'd reply that he was in the other room making *mammucielle*, little doodles of figures.

My interest in drawing made getting Johnny Christmas and birthday presents very easy. It was always crayons, paper, pencils. I drew constantly. Soldiers, airplanes, Mom, Dad, houses, horses, wagons. Sometimes I just filled in the lettering on Hearn or Loesser department stores ads. It seemed I just couldn't get enough of it.

By the time I was about twelve or thirteen, I knew what I wanted to do with all this drawing. My mother asked me if I was going to be a doctor or a lawyer. Her dream, again.

"I'm not gonna be a doctor or a lawyer, I'm gonna be a newspaper artist."

I had seen the magnificent political cartoons by Rollin Kirby in the old *New York World.* I had no idea that he was commenting on political affairs. But I knew that he drew beautifully and that his drawings were on display almost every day. What could be better than doing just that for the rest of your life?

I remember the shocked expression on Mom's face. "No docta? No lawya? *Tu ci pazze*—you crazy! Artist a starv!"

Since Mom was the fountainhead of all wisdom, I naturally assumed I was going to starve in my chosen profession. So I started practicing. At frequent intervals I would go a day or two without eating.

Mom used to hover over me and beg me to eat. "*Mange, figliu miu*—Eat, child of mine, for Mama."

I would resist stubbornly for a day or so until the fragrant aroma of meat sauce, spaghetti and meatballs got to me again. I never dug spaghetti too much but the meatballs and meat sauce were the chink in my armor.

I was in my last year at Alexander Hamilton High School in Brooklyn when I dropped out and started looking for work. It was time to go looking for work, because it was 1932, deep into the Depression. I wasn't quite sixteen. I remember doing the rounds of all the gloomy factories—a chocolate factory, a horn factory, a glue factory. God! The zombies going to work and feeling lucky as hell that they were working. I wanted to work desperately and yet thought how miserable it would be to get lucky and become a zombie for the rest of my life.

I'd look for work from six to about ten or eleven every day. Then I'd go to a candy store and hang around there with friends until we were chased away. Then we'd hang around outside until we were chased by the cop on the beat, then I'd go home and argue with my father, who thought I was becoming a bum.

Those arguments were so consistent and tiresome that finally I lit out in the dead of winter with three friends. We hopped a freight train out of

Jersey. Being novices we jumped into a gondola, which is an open freight car with sides three feet high but no roof.

We didn't know where we were going or how long it was going to take. We had frozen our balls off by the time the train stopped in a yard at Selkirk, New York, one hundred and fifty miles north of New York City. We jumped off the gondola into a couple of feet of snow, saw some lights ahead, and, frozen stiff, moved toward them.

We entered a large building that contained enormous turbines, and called out. No one answered. We walked around and finally came to a very large room which had a kitchen stove and cabinets at one end. We opened the cabinets and saw all these lovely cans of food. We were starving. We kept calling for someone and finally a guy showed up. He looked at this miserable bunch and wanted to know what we were doing there. We explained about our trip in the open gondola, and that we were looking for work. He said we must be hungry. He started cookings eggs and ham and soup and I thought he was the most wonderful guy in the world. We slept on the floor and he awakened us before his relief came early in the morning.

The weeks that followed found us riding freights, stopping in towns, looking for work, eating at Salvation Army kitchens and missions, and some-times being put up in cells by police for the night. There were thousands of young men and even older guys travelling like we were, and looking for work. Word got around where not to go: South—they put you in chain gangs down there. So we moved west from Albany: Syracuse, Rochester, Buffalo, Erie.

In Erie the police told us about the new transient camps President Roosevelt was setting up around the country for people like us. Hundreds of thousands of unemployed were shuffling around the country, back and forth, looking for work.

Actually the transient camp wasn't a camp at all. It was a large frame house. We were told the rules when we got there: take a shower immediately, go get a night shirt—one of these things you see in cartoons and old movies. They looked like ankle-length dresses. We were given three meals a day and there was no limit to how long we could stay. One day . . . three days . . . three months . . . .

Before breakfast, the entire house had to be cleaned. We drew floor-scrubbing assignments. That was it. The rest of the day was ours. We stayed four days and never found any more transient camps. In Cleveland we spent the night in a cell in a very large jail. Mission people came by in the morning singing hymns and passing out meal tickets.

We schlepped on to Chicago and Kenosha, Wisconsin, then back to New York City and Brooklyn. *This* time, I decided I'd get a job on a ship.

A friend of mine and I used to go to the docks on the Brooklyn waterfront all the time anyway. We brought sandwiches and sat on the barges, listening to the water slap-slapping against the sides of the barge. Just the up and down movement of the barge gave us the feeling we were out at sea.

Especially after our cross-country train touring, we wanted badly to get a job on a ship and see the hell out of the world. We haunted the docks and the guys guarding the gangplanks, asking everywhere for work. We were told that you had to show discharge papers from your last trip. Since we had never been to sea, how the hell could we show dismissal papers?

Someone one day pointed to a guy with a white Homburg and a tailored coat, picking his teeth, and told us we could get papers from him. We went up to him and he never looked at us, just kept jabbing at his teeth with the toothpick. We kept talking and finally, still without looking at us, said, "It'll cost y' twenny fi' bucks, stan' whad I mean?" Twenty-five bucks! That must've been half the dough in the world. We tried to get him down to half of that but it was "Stan' whad I mean, twenny fi'!"

My friend and I ran around hustling work, washing windows, hauling ashes, and delivering stuff, and weeks and weeks later, we went looking for "Stan' whad I mean" on the docks. He took our money and a week later he reappeared with papers. Mine had my brother's name on them, Enrico Fischetti, because I was too young. "Stan' whad I mean" had also talked to a guy and I had a job as engineer's messman on a Munson Steamship liner, the *Western World*. It carried freight and five hundred passengers to Bermuda and South America, then stopped in Barbados on the way back home, to refuel.

My job was to wait on table for about eight engineers, to keep their quarters clean, by polishing all the brass, portholes, knobs, water taps, and to make their beds.

We left New York about dinnertime so I was too busy to see much. After work I went to bed in a glory hole, a large compartment housing about eighteen men, with lower and upper bunks. I drew an upper.

The following morning, while walking to the engineers' quarters I glanced out of the porthole. I shouted, "Wow! Lookit that!" A couple of sailors leaped to look. I said, "Lookit the color of the water!" Shaking their heads, they walked on.

To me it was unbelievable. The water was Prussian blue. The only water I had seen before was near the docks, brownish, grayish green, and spotted here and there with condoms, known in Chicago as "Chicago trout."

But the freshness, the deepness, the clarity of the Prussian blue sea water! I felt like I was on another planet.

I loved every minute of the year I spent at sea. The incredibly clear Southern Cross in the heavens . . . the phosphorescent trail of the dolphin . . .the dolphins leaping and arching across the ship's bow . . .the skittering of flying fish . . . the absolutely thrilling plunge down and the breathtaking ups as the ship went through mountainous seas in a hurricane off Cape Hatteras . . . watching old Casey, a deck hand in his seventies, battening things down while hanging over the ship's side during the same storm . . . sitting in Casey's quarters watching him shave with a straight razor while the ship went up and down and rolled side to side . . . Old Casey fondling his gun and palming a handful of bullets, telling me that he was an atheist and that the gun was his god and the bullets were the disciples . . . watching the longshoremen in Santos ducking into the petty officers' quarters, ripping their clothes off and putting layer after layer of women's panties and bras on, putting their own

clothes back on and returning to shore carrying something plus their smuggled goods, then ducking into a shanty and divesting themselves of all the bras and panties . . . .

The *Western World* docked at the foot of Montague Street in the Heights section of Brooklyn. I walked down the gangplank carrying my small, cheap suitcase. I had about two hundred feet to go to the entrance of the pier. I loved the smell of spices and herbs that permeated the building on the pier. I saw Dad waiting for me. He insisted on carrying my suitcase and we started humping up the steep cobblestone street. I pulled out a cigarette and asked Dad if he wanted one. Surprised, he asked, "You smokin' now?" I dragged and said, "Sure," while blowing the smoke out. What the hell, I thought, I'm sixteen and a half and I've been to Bermuda, Santos, Montevideo, Buenos Aires, and Rio de Janeiro, where I got laid. On the way back to New York my ship stopped to refuel in Barbados, British West Indies, so I've been there, too. What the hell's this about smoking? Christ, what am I, a kid or something?!

I was kind of a hero to the family, relatives and friends since I was the only one to really leave the neighborhood. When I was a kid it was a helluva lot easier to be a hero. Just getting out of the neighborhood did it.

The next character-building job I got during the Depression was as a janitor-doorman at an apartment house on Ocean Parkway in Brooklyn. I mopped five or six stories of hallways, tended the furnace, hauled the ashes out and then cleaned up, as well as performed doorman duties. Twelve hours a day, seven days a week, ten bucks on the barrelhead each and every week.

One of the tenants was a hood who always seemed to have more than enough green. He also had a good-looking doll, who looked neither left nor right. Neither of them ever said hello, thanks or screw you.

Another tenant was Hymie Caplin, a man of about thirty-two, a prize-fight manager who used to give me tickets to see his tigers fight at Ridgewood Grove, a local sports arena.

They fought every Friday night and on Saturday morning they'd come to Hymie's apartment to explain why the nose was broken or the ear squashed or the eye multi-colored. Most of them were kids about eighteen or nineteen and I'd let these bandaged gladiators in to see Caplin, after calling on the hall phone.

One night Caplin came home a little tipsy, smoking a long expensive cigar, wearing a camel's hair coat. He greeted me with, "Hey, kid, you gotta good built, y' wanna be a fighter?"

I told him I had seen all his pugs coming to see him on Saturdays, with cotton in their noses, and banged ears and all looking as if Fred Astaire had used their heads as a platform to tap dance on.

On the other hand, I said, you smoke expensive cigars, you have a beautiful wife, two lovely kids, a big apartment, a maid and you got me opening doors for you, yet you never have a mark on you.

"Why don't you teach me how to be a manager?"

Hymie Caplin stared at me and said, "Oh, a smart Wop kid, hunh?"

26

PRATT

For several years during the Depression, I went to Pratt Institute to try to enroll. I had been vaguely aware of the place for years, since it was in the immediate neighborhood of our apartment on Greene Avenue. Pratt had an excellent library set in pretty park-like grounds, and it was a terrific place for a kid who loved books so much to spend a lot of time. I knew there was an "art school" back behind the library, but it didn't mean a thing to me. Then when I began to be serious about wanting to be a "newspaper artist," I realized I knew very little about how to do that or what it would be like, except that "Artist 'a starve!" as Mom said. I wasn't sure what one would do in an art school other than starve, but I knew that if they knew more about it than I did, it was the place for me.

As often as I went to enroll, they turned me down, because a high school diploma was one of the requirements. Miss Everest, the head of the Illustration Department, got to know me quite well, since I kept coming back and she kept turning me down. But finally she cracked, admitting me to Pratt in 1938 if I promised to finish my algebra and geometry courses at summer school. I promised, and for the next three years I kept flunking those goddamn algebra and geometry Regents tests in summer school, every year.

I had come to Pratt almost totally inexperienced in using any art medium other than the plain drawing pencil I used to make the sketches that so impressed my family. I had never even attempted to work with oils, watercolors or pastels, nor had I ever tried set or costume design or sculpting with any material. I had it all to learn.

I was a "neighborhood kid" and I guess it showed. During my first week at Pratt, I was proudly carrying the new art supplies I had just bought at the supply store on DeKalb Avenue. Under one arm I had a large folio containing drawing paper, and in that hand I had a little tin growler or pot of the kind

kids used to fetch beer for adults from saloons. I had done it myself when I was a kid. But this growler was to hold water in watercoloring class. My other hand held the handle of a kind of tin tool box with several different compartments filled with erasers, crayons, pencils, razor blades, the stumps used to smear pencil marks to get a shaded effect, assorted brushes, thumbtacks and all the other paraphernalia an art student would need.

I turned off DeKalb and walked with my burdens down Ryerson toward the school along with the general flow of student traffic. Then coming toward me away from the school I saw a guy named Sam Gilman, whom I had known for a couple of years in quite another context. He was a student at Pratt, but he used to get into the floating crap games a

couple of other guys from the neighborhood and I used to keep running. There were a few students who got into these games, and Sam was usually around either playing or watching. He only knew me as one of the neighborhood guys who ran the games. Period. I had certainly never told him about wanting to be an artist or going to Pratt. It just had nothing to do with shooting crap.

So when Sam saw me with all the art gear headed for Pratt, he was of course sure I was about to get a game going inside the school. He was stunned at the idea that I was a serious student. He'd had no idea that I had any talent of any kind, much less artistic, and he barely seemed to believe me even after I told him my intentions.

A tall guy who used to play basketball at Pratt, Sam's greatest interest even then was always the theatre, both in acting and directing. By the time I got to Pratt, he had graduated, but he stayed on for several years, directing plays and other theatre activities. And he did wind up acting, in TV and movies.

One day years later when I was walking through Penn Station on my way to NEA to do my political cartoons, I ran into Sam, who was with a very good-looking actress from California. He clapped me on the back and introduced me to his girl. Even then the first thing he told her about me was about the crap games, and that he *still* couldn't believe I was a professional cartoonist.

He became an actor, and I'm making a living from my art. But Sam's a hard man to convince.

Sam's doubts that I could possibly make it were well justified. At Pratt, you had to hustle all the time, because there were so many people with talent there. And there was plenty of outspoken criticism, a lot of which came from the teacher at Pratt who probably had the greatest effect on me, both as a man and an artist. I learned an incredible amount from my design teacher, Alexander Kostellow.

My first year as a student at Pratt was Kostellow's first year there as a teacher. He had taught at Carnegie Tech before Pratt.

On the first day, our whole class had to wait for some time before Kostellow appeared. He smiled as he entered, and in an accent which I believe was Persian, told us to draw a picture in pencil on a piece of notepaper and tack it on the wall the following day. Then he waved, turned and left. Puzzled, we gathered in groups and finally went to our next class. We thought he was really flaky.

The following day Kostellow appeared, smiling. He strolled along the wall, his hands behind his back, and looked at the drawings we all had dutifully tacked up.

He stopped and squinted at my drawing, turned around and asked, "Who's Feeshettee?"

I raised my hand. He stared at me, still smiling, and said, "I wouldn't deegneefy thees drawing weeth a creeteseesm."

I flushed, stood up and said, "What the hell d'you mean you won't dignify my work with a criticism? What are you here for?"

He lifted his brows, smiled wider and chortled, "Ah! Hee's got speerit!—Good! Good!"

In teaching us design for the next two years, he taught us how to think. He never drew or painted, but he'd get colossal arguments on design started. Then he'd sit back, smile and enjoy.

One day when he came in he said, "Feeshettee, I understand you do a wonderful eemeetation of me."

I was stunned. I didn't know he knew. He insisted on seeing the imitation. When I finally did it, he smiled very broadly and said, "Good! Good!"

Half the class hated Kostellow's tactics. They felt he was a talker, not a doer. But the other half of the class became his disciples, and I was one of them. For years after I left Pratt, I went back to the notes I had taken in his class and kept learning long after I had left him.

I remember the time at Pratt as one of working

incredibly hard, at least during the week: there was so much homework, so many assignments to do outside class, and I had so much ground to make up. One of the consequences of all the hard work was that almost all of our free time was spent knocking down huge quantities of beer. We had some prodigious times off campus, and many, many hours were spent at the German-American beerhall near Gramercy Park. The "G.A." to us.

One of the men sawed away on a violin. Another banged out tunes on a tinny piano. Their expressions were vacant and their moves mechanical. Clearly they had put in so many weekends like this for so many years.

It was just one enormous, smokey room filled with sweating, smoking, croaky-voiced students from Pratt, Yale, Columbia, Amherst, Harvard, Wellesley, Holyoke, Smith—nearly every place. Everyone was singing old school songs and the old favorites: "If you'll be m-i-n-e, mine, I'll be t-h-i-n-e, thine . . ." "We'll build a bunnnn-ga-lowwww for two . . ." or "You'll wear a toolip, a big yellow toolip, and I'll wear a big red ro-o-o-o-se . . ."

Singing, arguing, nuzzling your girl, swearing undying friendships, being let in on secret fraternity handshakes because you didn't belong to the fraternity, always forgetting the goddamn handshake since it wasn't at all important to begin with.

And Jesus, yes, saddle shoes, the badge of our years. The subway ride home, carrying Johnnie Donaldson over the turnstile, barfing in the corners of the subway station. We always looked forward to those nights at the G.A.

At other times we'd go to the Original Max'ls or the other German restaurants up and down 86th Street, in the Yorkville section of Manhattan.

We sang there, too. "Ist das nicht ein Schnitzelbank? Ja! Das ist ein Schnitzelbank! Und ist das nicht . . . " and everything down to the mother-in-law. The little suet-y German waiter who led us in the singing in his *lederhosen* would swat the appropriate canvas covered with the drawings and the lyrics as we accompanied him in song. He looked for all the world like one of Disney's three little pigs.

The war was going on in Europe in those days and there was a very active German-American Bund in New York, with all the trappings—the flags, the swastikas, the impressive, silvered, deep-dish drums. The Bund leader was Fritz Kuhn.

When we were going to these joints on 86th Street, Nazis were a joke—that clown in the mustache babbling away in German and ludicrously posturing. The evil, terror and filth of Hitler and his followers had not yet become apparent.

So we drank beer, sang Schnitzelbank and paid very little attention to a thin Goebbels-like regular who always sat at the last table in a corner of one restaurant. The waiters were constantly reporting to him, bowing slightly but stiffly, heels together. Not looking Schnitzelbanky at all. Later we learned that this man was one of the principal leaders of the Bund, and that these restaurants were where the news about the German community was both gathered and disseminated. It cast a strange light over our happy, drunken times in beerhalls.

The war came to affect us all, of course, especially one of my closest friends, Don Berry, a tall, black-haired, handsome guy from Hornell, New York. He was the first student I met at Pratt. After the first year there, you selected the course you were going to specialize in—illustration, advertising, teacher training, etc. When Don and I discussed the various courses, he said he wanted to go into advertising.

"Are you good at printing?" I asked.

"You don't call it printing when you letter by hand, it's called lettering." I've never forgotten that encounter, nor my friend Don.

But he was kind of a star-crossed guy. Don worked his butt off at school waiting on tables, doing janitorial work and living in a house crammed with art students. The more students they crammed into the house, the lower the monthly rent. I think Don told me that he and his housemates finally got it down to two bucks a month.

After three lean years at school, Don got a job in an advertising agency. After graduation he wrote to me in California, where I was holding down my first job with Walt Disney Studios, to exult about how terrific it was to have a couple of coins to rub together. But it didn't last long.

Don, like most of us, was drafted in World War II and became an Infantry lieutenant. My last year in the Army, while I was on *Stars and Stripes,* Don saw some of my drawings in the paper and wrote to me. He enclosed his unit patch and told me to write as soon as possible, saying he had been in combat for some time and had a feeling that he was going to get it, and soon. My letter came back unopened. It was marked "Deceased" and signed by his Company Commander. Later, on assignment in Germany, I made inquiries about Don. He had gotten it in the first German town the Allies took, Aachen. Don was buried in a military cemetery in Maastricht, Holland.

One of two students who had a lifelong effect on me was Lenny Karsakov, who was a senior when I was a freshman. Lenny was a terrific illustrator and worked remarkably well in watercolors and in oils. He did many book illustrations and all his work had a real style: you could tell if something had been done by Lenny. Fortunately for us, Lenny was not only creative and talented, but was a natural teacher as well. In addition, he was one of the funniest guys I've ever met, a natural comedian, so it was always a delight to have him around.

We all used to go out watercoloring in Brooklyn, down by the docks, then up around Springfield, Massachusetts, where Lenny was from, doing barns and covered bridges. We also painted in Provincetown, at the tip of Cape Cod, doing skeletal shipwrecks, the dunes, and the wonderful narrow winding streets in the town.

I can remember once when we were out doing watercolors of barns and covered bridges in New England. I quickly drew this red barn and thought I was finished. Then Lenny came up behind me and said, "Jesus, Johnnie, you're not looking at that barn! That's not what's there at all." "What do you mean?" "Johnnie, look at the *color* of that barn— it's not red. There's green in it, see by the eaves? And there's a lot of brown, and some blue." It was one of the first occasions when I felt I was beginning to understand color. Suddenly it took the whole afternoon to do that barn.

On another afternoon when Lenny and I were returning from watercoloring, we realized we were near a camp we'd been told about. We knew nothing about the place except that the brother of a friend of ours had told us about it and said that he belonged to it.

We decided to stop by, and once we were there, it didn't take long to get the picture: everybody was calling everybody else "Comrade." If you didn't know the other person's name it was plain "Comrade;" otherwise, if you did know, it was "Comrade Joe" or "Comrade Daisy."

But they were glad to see us and gave us each a pair of shorts and told us to go into one of a line of little shacks about eight by eight to change. When we got inside the place pointed out to us, there were both young men and women in various stages of undress, changing. At the time, free love and not making a big deal about the naked body was very prevalent in the Communist movement. So Lenny and I changed to the shorts, ogling the young women slyly and trying to appear nonchalant. We tried to remember a little of the "Internationale" and hum snatches of it. Lenny leered at me and I leered back at him, covertly.

Out on the playing fields, everything was fun and games. The Nazis and the Communists were emphasizing the "Body Beautiful" during those years. The newsreels always showed them in shorts, bronzed bodies glistening in the sunlight, marching down a road carrying shovels, or building more roads so they could show more of them carrying shovels, other bodies glistening in the sunlight. In Italy, that bullet-headed shnook Mussolini was always stripped to the waist, going through fiery hoops or rings of bayonets and exhorting his followers to do the same.

So back at this camp in the upstate New York countryside, Lenny and I flexed our flat feet and jogged over to where a volleyball game was in progress. We joined the game, and Lenny, never too athletic, promptly lost a point for his side by missing the ball. When he lost a second point, the guy near him, a fierce competitor, began to shout at him, "I've got it, Comrade!" whenever the ball came close to Lenny. Lenny ignored him and blew that one, too. Super-jock screamed "I've got it, Comrade!" again the next time, but Lenny got there first and lost yet another point. Just before we left Lenny lost the last point, and by that time, old Fierce-ass was Red-ass, and bellowing, "F' Chrisssake!!! Comrade!"

We changed clothes, got a sandwich, and went home to mat our watercolors. Our political education was slow but fairly direct in those days.

Lenny was one of the few students in our group in those days who had any political consciousness; we were all remarkably naive politically. Certain things were clear but didn't seem political as such. When a teacher assigned the class to do illustrations for any book of our choice, I found that I naturally always chose something about the poor, the unfortunate, the put-upon. I saw the crummy places these people lived in and that not many people really cared about them. I grew to hate injustices and the people responsible for these injustices. Steinbeck was very important to me, and at one point I carefully did a complete set of illustrations for the *Grapes of Wrath*.

I also spent a lot of time doing illustrations for a book called *Christ in Concrete* by Pietro di Donato. Donato, a construction worker, told the story of his father, who'd been a construction worker before him, and who'd been hurled into the wet concrete below when part of a building under construction collapsed because of the shoddy materials the contractor was using. I sketched a picture of his father's hand sticking up in a pool of wet concrete as his corpse slowly sank. The building was completed right over his father's body which was never recovered. Di Donato's uncle lost a leg in another construction accident. Di Donato wrote with an anger I felt totally in sympathy with about how the

tragedies did not even affect the construction schedules, but only the powerless workers and their families. The work I did on that project was later to land me a job.

But somehow I never thought of calling these convictions political and any more active role just didn't occur to me. Students did not march in protest against government policies in those days as they do now. Now at nine or ten, kids of our friends are aware of Vietnam, Daniel Ellsberg and the Watergate. But for us in the 1940s, it started with a social consciousness, which for me was born out of where I grew up.

After Pratt, Lenny's gift for teaching found an unexpected outlet. He went to Washington, D.C., and began to work for the Public Health Service under a guy named Bob Schmuck. Together, they designed and illustrated the first educational campaign about venereal disease. They set up traveling exhibits and took them around the country. Lenny and Bob Schmuck—who later changed his name to Thorpe—really are responsible in large part for our being able to mention the term VD without causing gasps and genteel fainting.

Funny start for a guy who's now the Art Director of a successful Boston advertising agency.

C. E. Monroe, Jr., or "Ed" to us, one of two Southerners in our group, was already a trained artist when he arrived at Pratt. He was in my class and was one of the most talented students Pratt has ever had.

His dad owned a letterhead company in Huntsville, Alabama, and his father meticulously drew the emblems and illustrations that were printed with the company names at the top of stationery. The work was always beautifully drawn. Ed's father trained him in perspective, drawing, color, and the use of various mediums from pen and ink to scratchboard to watercolor. The senior Monroe was a fine craftsman who simply wouldn't put up with shoddy work, and Ed learned the various techniques from him very well.

Ed was a tall, slim, blonde with an enormous amount of poise for a young man in the big city for the first time. His resemblance to the movie actor, Franchot Tone, his easy charm and his slow Southern accent were not lost on Yankee girls. He was very attractive to women, and attracted by them as well.

He was generous as hell with his knowledge, and willingly took a lot of time showing the rest of us how to handle various mediums, how to check and correct perspective, and design and construction of figures.

A sociable guy and a talented musician who learned by ear since he didn't read music, he loved to sing with a group which several guys from Pratt formed, and to play his guitar. But he was also a little lazy. I can still picture him strumming his guitar, his long legs stretched out across his bed when I'd arrive in the mornings to pick him up on my way to school. I would hustle in, having slaved all the previous night to get an assignment right while he would indicate he was going to throw it together just then if I'd only wait a minute. He once observed that if he had my stick-to-itiveness he might amount to something. I always had the feeling he'd do "right well" just doing what he was doing, and he has.

After leaving Pratt, Ed did illustrations for *Life, Colliers,* and other leading magazines, and also did a lot of work for book publishers in the South. Now living in Chase, a suburb of Huntsville, he free-lances covers and illustrations for *True* and *Field and Stream* magazines, does portraits on commission, and owns and runs a small art gallery together with his wife.

He is one of several men from Pratt who married other artists, and it is interesting to me to note that over the last thirty years, these are the marriages that have stood up and seem to have been the happiest. Perhaps artists are not the most mad and unstable group after all.

Betty, his wife, who was a very talented student at Pratt with us, has portrait commissions lined up for the next three years. They have a son, and their daughter, at twenty-three, is said to have enough talent to eventually become one of the very best fine art painters in America. Ed has done just fine.

In those days at the G.A., our own German was Bob Kuhn—of no relation to the Bund leader, Fritz. A blond, round-faced guy, his physical appearance was deceiving. Because of his round head, one tended to think of him as round, but he had swum competitively in high school and had the big shoulders and smooth flowing muscles of a champion swimmer. It was always a surprise, in intramural baseball and football, to discover how fast he was.

In the summers, he loved to go out West where the animals were. He always had a passionate interest in sketching, painting and doing anatomical research on animals. He *never* stopped doing it, and he was wonderful at it. I used to kid him about his western safaris, and so we got nicknames for each other from that. We still use them when we run into each other. He's "Mesquite" and I'm "Cactus."

Mesquite Kuhn couldn't get into the service during the war because of flat feet or something, and so he got a job in the Merchant Marine, where he manned one of the guns on his ship all during the war.

But he went back to where he left off after that. He, too, married a woman who'd been an excellent student at Pratt, although Libby doesn't work anymore—at least not at art. But Bob continued his work, and I've always considered him one of the best animal artists in the country. A protégé of Paul Bransom's, Bob has stopped working for magazines and now paints game animals on commission. He has very successful shows in galleries out West.

Ed Monroe and Bob Kuhn both had wonderful singing voices, and together with two other Pratt students they used to perform as a sort of informal quartet. Some of the rest of us used to join in, especially at the German American, but we were mainly awful. It's funny to think of that diverse group together now; they've gone in quite different directions.

De Wolfe Hotchkiss or Hotch or Hop or Hopper was the third member of the quartet. He now lives in Gaylordsville, Connecticut, with his wife Grace. An advertising major then, Hotch now runs a small ad agency in Sherman, Connecticut, while Grace runs the basket shop they own. They have four boys, of which two are Pratt graduates like Hotch, so maybe talent can be inherited.

Ed Ahlmgren, the Swede in our crowd, from New Haven, Connecticut, was the fourth part of the musical group. Another advertising major who really made it, he's now a top advertising executive in New York City, as the Head Art Director and Vice-President of Batten, Barton, Durstine, Osborn.

There were others who were an important part of those days, who still turn up frequently now. I suppose in other circles it could be called "old school ties." Elmer Wexler, better known as "Red," was really considered cool when we were all students at Pratt. A senior when we were freshmen, he actually *sold* stuff! A marvelous illustrator, in his last year at Pratt, he did work for *Argosy, Blue Book* and other first rate pulp magazines. A terrific illustrator, he worked as a Marine combat correspondent during the war, and did numerous spreads for *Life* afterward. In spite of his success as an illustrator, he then turned himself into a one-man advertising agency where he lives in Weston, Connecticut. Now a successful businessman, he comes into Chicago every three months or so for one of his clients, and so we get to see each other often. It's not totally unlikely, but no one would have pictured Red as a businessman.

Johnnie Donaldson was a really good-looking guy with a lot of talent from Westchester County, just outside New York. He married his girl from the Pratt days, Ann; they moved to Washington, and he began to illustrate pamphlets for the Navy. Johnnie always loved the outdoors, though, and the country, and dogs. He and Ann live in the Virginia countryside outside Washington now, and Johnnie spends as much time and loving attention on breeding dogs as he does on his job with the Navy. I guess it has become close to a full-time occupation for him.

Then there are several people, all of whom were just as talented as any of the rest of us, and who worked as hard and seemed just as serious about art, who ended up quite far afield. Al Aquino, a big man still called Moose, and his wife Ann Cobb were both tremendously talented students who attended Pratt with us, but for years they have been running a tack shop for the horsey set in Redding, Connecticut.

Paul Eckley was a tall guy who was an excellent runner in track who was an illustration major along with Ed Monroe, Johnnie Donaldson and myself. His father was a coach at Amherst and so we all used to go to games and athletic events there and sleep in his parents' attic. Inexplicably, Paul stayed in the service after the war and I think he retired as a colonel.

One Pratt graduate who stayed in art and did me an important favor a few years later was Al Avison, the prolific one—I've never seen anyone draw as fast or as well as he. In the days right after World War II he used to work so furiously, constantly puffing on a cigar, that he never had time to cash the checks that kept piling up on his desk. The agencies were always calling to get him to cash the checks; he fouled up their books.

One of the first times I ran into Al was when we were playing a pick-up game of touch football at the Pratt athletic field. Al, a skinny little shit of about one hundred and twenty, was lined up opposite my one hundred and eighty. When the play was called, Al tossed a handful of dirt in my face. Our friendship could only go uphill after that. And it did.

After the war Al and I often double-dated or just had drinks together at different places, Costello's, P. J. Clarke's or Bleeck's.

Then in 1948 he ran into a Danish actress while out in the country fishing or some unlikely thing, and they started going together. One night a few months later he called me at my apartment on 44th Street to say that he was at his girl friend's birthday party, that everyone there was Danish, it was a gas, and I should hustle right over to join them. I was working on two or three free-lance jobs that night at once, and the deadlines on all three were the next morning. So I told Al I couldn't make it, that with these deadlines I'd be up all night anyway.

Al usually didn't call back to insist when he had

something going for us both and I said "no" or that I was busy. But fortunately that night he was persistent and kept calling until, to get him off my back, I agreed to run up for a fast drink. The party was only two blocks away, at 46th and Lexington. I met my wife Karen there that night for the first time.

My very first question was, "Are you married?" and the answer was "No." I discovered that this beautiful woman was a stewardess with SAS, the Scandinavian Airline System, who had asked for six months of ground duty after almost three years of flying. She was then working as a passenger agent, and the six months was almost up. I enjoyed the party for a while, made another date with Karen, and then went back to my apartment and my three deadlines.

I saw Karen often after that. Then one day I was in Al's room at the Webster Hotel with Sam Gilman and his date, a Swiss tightrope dancer. I was supposed to meet Karen there, and when she showed, she looked so good next to the tightrope dancer that I walked her out to Bryant Park near the public library at 42d and Fifth Avenue and proposed. She accepted and six weeks after we had first met we were married.

The omens were not exactly all in favor of that occurring. After my proposal, one of Karen's closest friends, another stewardess named Anna, who'd been in the Danish underground during the war, told Karen she'd like to meet with me alone. Karen had no objections, and Anna and I met in the bar of the Henry Hudson Hotel, the place where the SAS crews always stayed between flights. She then gave me a thousand reasons why Karen and I shouldn't get married. She was and is Karen's best friend and didn't want to see Karen get hurt. I listened to all of Anna's arguments but paid no attention to them, proving that I was as impetuous and headstrong as she suspected, I suppose.

That was only bested by Karen's mother's remark, "I wonder how long *that* will last?"

On the first day after that which Karen could get off, we went to Elkton, Maryland, and got married. With her best friend's doubts, her mother's jaundiced remarks and my having to borrow the dough for the ring from Karen herself, I'm surprised she went through with it.

We've been married twenty-five years this October 25th and will celebrate our anniversary in Copenhagen and Silkeborg, Denmark. I still don't see what she sees in me but I certainly still do see what I've always seen in her.

Despite all the good times and good friends at Pratt, about two or three months before graduating, I decided to take off and move to California. I think that year, when I was twenty-three and in my last year at Pratt and my first year as a working professional, is the closest I can come to pinpointing the time when I first knew I wanted to be a political cartoonist, not just a newspaper illustrator. By then, I had found out that politics was the linchpin of most of the social ills I had seen. I'd discovered that a good politician was worth his weight in gold, and that I should therefore make the bad politicians my targets. To me, those were the guys protecting the interests of the wealthy, the greedy and the opportunists over the needs and aspirations of the millions.

I had always found myself gravitating naturally toward the artists, writers, journalists, ministers and others who wanted more out of life than a bigger bag of loot at someone else's expense. I was a young idealist then, and I hope to die an idealist. But by that time I had decided that I could contribute most with my political cartoons.

I was doing some illustrations for poems written by Bettie Sale for Rob Wagner's *Script.* Wagner knew my aspirations and sent me to Manchester Boddy, the publisher of a liberal tabloid in Los Angeles. When I talked to him, Boddy said he thought I'd make a good political cartoonist some day, but he didn't hire me. It was the only lead I had, so God knows how I thought I was going to support myself.

Fortunately a few days after arriving in Los Angeles, I ran into Jules Svenson, whom I had known at Pratt, who suggested that I come over to take the test to be an artist at the Walt Disney Studios, where he worked. I did, I passed, and for about eight months I sketched away. Then, for the first time, I started to have trouble with my eyes. Whether it was working all day staring into the large bulb of a light board or putting lines in between two different drawings, I never did find out, but I had to take about two months off.

One grew to hate working at Disney's. It was an assembly line for artists. In a sense, you were just turning your one nut and then starting on another, but with your pencil instead of a wrench.

When you're drawing the "in-betweening" which is what I was doing, the monotony is deadly. In-betweening is drawing line for line all the lines in between two completely drawn but different positions to produce an animated cartoon figure.

Two of my fellow assembly line sufferers there were Jimmy Pinto and John Dehner. After thirty years, those friendships, forged at the oars of the galley ship at Disney's, continue to this day.

Jimmy Pinto is a fine artist, painting and teaching painting at the Instituto de San Miguel de Allende in Mexico. He sells his paintings and has successful shows all over the world.

John Dehner has been an actor since then. He began with newscasting, later went into TV acting, and now does movies. He's very talented and loves what he's doing now. He just finished "Day of the Dolphin" with George Scott, a film directed by Mike Nichols which will be released in 1973.

Off to a hateful start, it's a pleasure to see that we escaped and have each been doing for many years what we do best and love the most.

I returned to Disney after my bout with the eye trouble but it had scared me, so I moved on to San Francisco, again without a job. It was a real hand-to-mouth time, with one exception: I ran into a guy from the Shell Oil Building, who thought the drawings I had done illustrating the *Grapes of Wrath* by Steinbeck were so good that he wanted to stage a show of them in the street window. While they were up there, a friend of Steinbeck's called me, saying he'd seen my work in the window and told Steinbeck about it, who wanted me to come right down to Carmel to show them to him. Needless to say, I yanked my stuff out of the window and took off for Carmel. Good God, Steinbeck himself!

In Carmel, I was pleasantly surprised to find that Steinbeck was a much bigger, burlier man than I'd expected, sandy-haired and hearty. He demanded that we proceed immediately to get a couple of cases of beer before going over my drawings, and

several hours later, it was, "Johnny boy!" and "Such talent!"

Still expansive, he called New York to insist that his publisher use my sketches in a new limited edition of *Grapes* which was then in process. When Steinbeck informed me sorrowfully that I had lost out to Thomas Hart Benton, one of my heroes, who was already under contract to illustrate the book, I could only roar, "Hey, man, that's the big time!"

So I trundled back to San Francisco, not having sold a thing, but as exultant as if it were the greatest triumph of my life.

However, despite the spiritual lift, things did not improve financially in San Francisco, so I made my way to Chicago, one of the cities I hadn't tried yet. There I had to work out a game plan: work my way up from the bottom somewhere, or strike for the top right away. Of course I decided to go out on a limb. *Esquire* was only around the corner from where I was staying, and Pietro Di Donato, whose book, *Christ in Concrete,* I had illustrated at Pratt, knew the Editor in Chief, Arnold Gingrich. Gingrich had discovered Di Donato and encouraged him to publish *Christ in Concrete,* which had run in *Esquire* first and had been a huge success, so I figured I had a chance. I brazenly called up, asked for Gingrich, and was suddenly faced with the man himself. A week or so later, I found myself doing illustration and spots for *Coronet,* which was published by the same company, and occasionally I did things for *Esquire.*

I figured it was the big time although I didn't seem to be making much money. At one point, I did a double page spread for *Esquire,* for which I was paid $15. Apparently, the editors figured "It was a showcase for the kid," and I was eager enough to be glad for it. That was when I really became friends with Bernie Lewis, who was an editor there at the time. He was so ashamed at the $15 fee that he offered me another $35 out of his own pocket. After the war, Bernie and I roomed together in New York.

At those prices, I still wasn't making it, so I began to work as an illustrator for the *Chicago Sun* in its pre-publication stage. Shortly thereafter, I found myself drawing in the office I shared with Albert Hubbell, Book Editor of the *Sun* and his assistant, Augie Spectorsky. One day an unexplained man walked in and started poking through my things. Indignantly, I wondered who the hell he was.

When he finally came up to me and asked if he could go through my portfolio, I said, "Why the hell not, since you've scrounged through everything else here?" He didn't seem to notice my testiness, and continued sifting through my stuff.

Then a young copy boy who happened to be in the office at the time and had seen the whole transaction blurted out an introduction. "Mr. Fischetti, I'd like you to meet Mr. Frank Taylor. Mr. Taylor is the Assistant to the Publisher."

I simmered down a bit and Taylor came over to say he liked my work very much. He asked me what ambitions I had in the illustration field, and of course I replied that I wanted to be a political cartoonist. Taylor nodded, and asked me if I could do two or three political cartoons in the next few days and bring them down to his office when they were ready. I certainly could!

I broke my butt for the next three days doing political cartoons, and turned out ten of them. Then I matted them carefully—even a bedbug would look good matted—and put some tissue over the drawings. First class presentation style. I called Taylor and told him the political cartoons he'd asked me to do were ready. He said to come on down.

Once in his office, I put all ten of the matted drawings up against the baseboard. He seemed overwhelmed. "Did you do all ten of these in the past three days?"

I said yes. It didn't occur to me until years later that as management, he was probably as impressed with my productivity as with the content of my drawings. But whichever it was, he said I'd hear from him.

A few days later my phone rang, and Turner Catledge, the Editor of the *Chicago Sun,* was on the other end of the line. "Mr. Fischetti, I've seen the political cartoons you drew. Would you please come to my office."

Catledge rose with his hand extended when I entered, shook my hand and said, "Congratulations! You are now the Associate Political Cartoonist on the *Chicago Sun.*" He told me my work would appear on the Op-Ed page.

I couldn't believe it. Bells rang, the earth shook. It was just like what happened when Ingrid Bergman crawled into the sleeping bag with Gary Cooper in "For Whom the Bell Tolls." It was what I had wanted from the time I was a kid, and it was happening.

I had arrived in Chicago in 1941. I didn't know a soul so I had gone to the Lawson Y.M.C.A. and rented a room by the day until I could find a place to rent by the week.

Walking all over the town, I thought that the near north side looked nice. There were quiet tree-lined streets—Chestnut, Oak, Bellevue, Cedar, Division— and the lake was nearby. It would be pleasant if I could find a small room along here in which to free-lance.

I picked up a newspaper and, scanning the near north possibilities, I saw a room for five dollars a week on the *Gold Coast*! Lake Shore Drive! I couldn't believe it! Imagine, me at my drawing board looking out at the lake from time to time! Unbelievable!

The address was 1240 North Lake Shore Drive. It was a large old mansion that the original wealthy owners had sold, and through the years it had changed hands until now it was kind of a genteel gloomy pile.

Excited, I rang the bell and informed the woman who opened the door that I was answering the ad about the room she had to rent.

Pleasantly, she told me to come in. I entered and saw this very wide, ornately carved, sweeping wooden staircase. Even at this late date, it looked elegant. I followed the woman up the long staircase. She paused for breath up at the top and I looked to my left. There was a room with an enormous open door, through which I could see the lake!

I asked the woman if that was the room for rent. She said "Oh no! It's down that way," and she pointed toward the right. Half-way down the long corridor she stopped, opened a door, and said this was it.

It wasn't even a room looking out at backyards. She turned on a light, which didn't do anything for the room because now you could see it. There were two small, narrow beds, one on each side of the

room and a window in the center. I pulled up the shade and found a brick wall two feet away. It was an air shaft.

She told me I had to share the room with a man who wasn't there much. He had a job inspecting fire sprinklers in offices and factories all over Illinois.

I was terribly disappointed, but I took the room, planning to find something better soon.

About a week later I did find a small room nearby on the fifth floor of a rooming house on Cedar Street. My room was just large enough for my bed and my drawing board. It cost five dollars a week but my window this time looked out on a very pleasant, tree-lined, quiet street.

The place I moved into had two round blue lights at the entrance. There were four houses together. The doors of three of the houses were sealed shut and the only one used was the one with the two blue lights outside. It was 61 East Cedar Street, called The Canterbury House, and a silver-haired couple, Mr. and Mrs. Madsen, owned it. They had a slow-moving, white English bulldog named Jerry.

Canterbury House was absolutely honeycombed with tiny, single rooms. The tenants were either young and on the way up (there was a lot of talent there—singing, modeling, painting), or older folks on the way down.

One could find a great deal of sexual activity there and quite often one didn't get back to one's own room for a week at a time . . . to sleep, that is. One did have to work.

Looking back, my first time around in Chicago was quite fine, indeed. I sold my work to major magazines for the first time. I got my first newspaper job and I had my first chance to do what I had wanted to do for a long time—my first political cartoons. I had made many friends. I loved Chicago and I was sorry to leave.

I had only been in Chicago about six months when Pearl Harbor intervened, and although I continued to work at the *Sun* for several months more, I felt very strongly that I belonged in that war.

I tried the Navy, the Marines, and the Army, and got physically thrown out each time because my eyes were a laughing matter to those guys. Finally, though, the draft board, unknowing, called me up for my physical. The examining physician didn't believe me when I said I couldn't read the large letter in the center of the eye chart; he'd seen too many malingerers. So we had it out.

"Look, Doc, I've been trying to get into this goddamn war for months now, and I keep getting rejected because of my eyes. If you just pass me on this, I know I can pass everything else."

"You mean it?"

"You bet your sweet ass!"

So although I had had a lot of fun in that old house on Cedar Street which had been a happy home for half a year or so, I said goodbye one morning at six a.m. and was inducted into the Army.

46

THE ARMY

The first part of my military career consisted of a long series of shifts from camp to camp throughout the States.

It was while I was stationed at Fort Meade, Maryland, that I started to get sore throats quite frequently.

A comrade of mine named Woody from Bakersfield, California, seemed to have the same trouble, so we went on sick call together one morning. We were told that we should have our tonsils out but since they were inflamed we should come back on sick call to have it done after the inflammation had subsided.

We did just that and wound up in a convoy of about twenty soldiers being wheeled down flat out and high from some drug being given. I was conscious, but I felt drunk and kept up a running conversation with Woody, who was in the wheeled stretcher in front of me.

We came to a large room, and were helped off the stretchers and seated back to back, ten on each side, in wire-backed chairs, the kind you sit in while you wait to get a haircut in a barber shop. We were wearing white gowns and little white caps, the kind doctors wear in the movies.

Little pans were handed to each one of us. When the doctor clipped my tonsils, he was to drop them in the pan I held. I never did find out.

A doctor seated himself in front of me and told me to open my mouth. He then proceeded to inject Novocain, one shot in the upper right part of my throat, two in the upper left, three in the lower right, when everything started to get fuzzy and swim around. I remember telling the doctor to hold my pan, as my voice got weaker and weaker and his head spun faster and faster before me, until I blacked out.

When I came to, a lot of sweating medics were holding me down and the doctor's anxious, perspiring face was right in front of mine. He had a hypodermic needle poised over my chest. An oxygen mask was held tightly over my nose and mouth.

When they saw my eyes open, everyone relaxed. The medics loosened their grip on me. The doctor was visibly relieved. He put down the needle and asked me how I felt. I said fine and then asked, what happened?

He told me to take some more whiffs of whatever was coming through the mask he had been holding over my nose and mouth.

After a short while, they wheeled me back to the ward, where I discovered that everyone's tonsils were gone except mine.

They told me I was allergic to Novocain and that I had had a heart reaction and convulsions, and that I had damned near died.

I was told I was going to have to wear a third dog-tag now. We always wore two dog-tags, with our name, religion, blood type, and serial number. Now my third dog-tag carried a warning that I was allergic to Novocain and that I'd suffer a heart reaction and convulsions if I was given any.

My friend Woody, his tonsils neatly clipped, went back to our outfit. I stayed on.

I was quite a curiosity. Doctors from all over Fort Meade came in to look at me. They kept their distance and among their whispered conversations I'd overhear "allergic," "convulsions," and the more mundane "tonsils."

My doctor, a fellow named Brock, a major, told me they were going to go in after those li'l ol' tonsils again, only this time I was going to have ether.

The turnout of observers in the operating room was pretty good—Hell! This guy could be allergic to ether, too!

The mask went over my face, and the anesthetist, a comely young nurse, told me to count backwards from 100—99, 98, 97, 96, 95—a big roar, 94—a railroad track with a single train wheel coming toward me faster and faster, another pair of tracks with a locomotive coal car and cars—the two made a V meeting right where I was. As they roared closer and closer, I yelled, "They're gonna hit an' right where I am."

I heard the nurse's voice fading away. . . .

I woke up later in the ward, without my tonsils, and at the mercy of all the other patients in the ward.

It seems that when you're coming out of ether you do what people command you to do. The guys shouted, "You're a truck driver!" "Turn right!" "Turn left!"

I was sitting up, dazed, groggy—obeying the commands . . .

"Your brakes! Your brakes! Step on 'em!"
"Back up! Shift gears!"
"Turn left! left! left!"

In my twilight-conscious state, I strained to obey. I was soaked with perspiration.

A nurse came in, scolded the men and dried me off. She changed my pajamas. I fell asleep. When I woke up, I felt like hell. The nurse remarked that I looked like hell, too, She left and returned with a doctor. One of my lungs had collapsed so they gave me a paper bag to blow up, empty, blow up, empty, and so on. I did this till I ran out of gas. I rested awhile and repeated the process.

The following day the nurse told me I *really* looked like hell. She called the doctor. After being examined, I was moved to another ward where the beds were encircled with white curtains. I could barely breathe.

Later on, they informed me I had developed pneumonia at this stage. About an hour after I was transferred, a nurse rolled in a machine about three feet high and two feet square with a lot of dials and indicators on a sloping dashboard. A hose wedded the machine to a rubber nose and mouth cone.

The nurse smiled brightly and covered my nose and mouth with the rubber cone. Carbon dioxide and oxygen were supposed to be coursing through my respiratory system from the machine at this point. Nothing. I shook my head. The nurse mistook this for a refusal to cooperate. She pressed the cone to my nose and mouth harder. The more I shook my head, the harder she clamped down. I was suffocating.

I gathered what strength I had left, tore the cone away from my face and cursed at the young lady. Her eyes opened wide, she was hurt and humiliated at my language. She dropped the cone, started to cry and bolted away.

She returned with a doctor, a captain, who chewed me out for cursing at a lieutenant. I motioned to him to come close. I was so weak, I could hardly tell him what happened, how nothing was coming out of the infernal machine and I was suffocating.

He questioned the nurse and found out she didn't know how to operate the machine; it was her first time with the thing and she had failed to turn it on.

She apologized, I apologized, the doctor showed her how to operate it properly. I finally took my first step toward recovery.

By the time I was fully recovered, a month and a half had gone by, and my outfit had left Fort Meade, Maryland, for Camp Crowder, Missouri, where I rejoined them, without my tonsils.

Finally my chance arrived to get closer to the action, as my outfit, the 999th Signal Corps, left New York City on a troopship bound for Scotland on a dreary, rainy day in February.

Red Cross girls served us hot coffee and doughnuts while we sat on our duffle bags on the dock. Finally it was our turn, and we staggered up the gangplank under all our gear.

Reaching the main deck we were instructed to go below—and below and below. The bunks were three or four high with about two feet of space in between mattresses. The crap games started before anybody even unpacked, and it started to stink even before we had worked up a sweat.

Having been to sea when I went to South America ten years before as a kid I began to wonder what it would be like when we got underway and guys started to barf. It didn't take long. One of my neighbors, a staff sergeant, started in before we were past Ambrose Lightship and didn't quit until they took him off on a stretcher in Greenoch, Scotland.

We joined a convoy, and were only allowed on deck after precautions about not letting lights show and not dumping litter overboard. The sight was unbelievable. I had never seen so many ships; they stretched from the horizon forward to the horizon aft. An aircraft carrier was behind us, loaded with planes, packed closely together, wings folded. But this carrier wasn't a fighter, it was just a carrier: the planes were being shipped to England. To our left and right, there were tankers low in the water, loaded with gasoline and oil.

The enlisted men and non-coms had the usual chow lines down below. Six or seven guys behind the counter dumping all the goodies on your mess kit so that you had a Jackson Pollock mélange of stew, stewed tomatoes, potatoes, peas and custard, all struggling for identity on the tin. It was so appealing that a lot of the guys couldn't make it to the long picnic tables. They just flew up to the promenade deck, hoping to make it in time.

The stronger stomachs, going up to the promenade deck at a more leisurely pace, had a view of the officers' dining room, replete with table cloths, china, silver and even serviettes.

Except for the fact that fuel oil, instead of water, was coming out of the six showerheads, things were uneventful until we were about halfway to Scotland.

My boat station was up forward on the starboard side of the ship right next to the cargo hatch. My boat was not a boat, it was a raft.

On St. Patrick's Day 1944, the ship's horn blew for boat drill. We knew it was a drill and soldiers were slowly going up the stairs to their boat stations. Black troops were quartered on the port side of the ship; my company was quartered on the starboard side. Blacks and whites converged at the stairs. In our own inimitable democratic fashion, there was a scuffle and some punches were thrown. Word of this reached the captain of the ship who misinterpreted what went on. He thought we were all scrambling in fear to get up to the deck.

When we reached our stations, the skipper thought he'd set this mob of landlubbers straight on the construction of a ship: "If a torpedo hits this ship we have watertight bulkheads; the doors will shut off the compartment that's hit. There is ample time to get off if we are seriously damaged."

We were dismissed, and my buddy, a fellow named Glose from Warren, Ohio, and I wandered up to the promenade deck. We had nicknamed each other Moldy, for obvious reasons, since we boarded this tub.

Leaning on our elbows we watched the tankers on our right. We noticed belching black smoke coming out of the stack of a corvette racing in the opposite direction from the convoy. Just as it reached the other side of the tanker on our right, the tanker was hit. An enormous fire ball flared and three-quarters of the vessel disappeared, leaving the last quarter of the ship at a ninety-degree angle. It turned toward our ship, then turned again, away from the convoy and slipped out of sight. The whole thing happened in a few minutes.

Every ship's horn in the convoy started bellowing. We all ran to our boat stations. It started to rain. I started to shake. My buddy, standing next to me, asked:

"Moldy, are you scared?"

Hoping he wasn't aware of my shaking, I said, "I don't know whether it's the cold or fear, but I'm shaking."

"Fuck that shit, I'm scared," Glose said.

After all the jazz about watertight bulkheads and time to stroll to your stations, the passengers were a little apprehensive, to put it mildly.

We were instructed to remain at our boat stations. When feeding time rolled around, we went in squads to the galley a few decks below.

All sprint records were broken, I'm sure, as guys galloped down, had their mess kits filled, and galloped back to the boat stations. No one wanted to be below decks, watertight bulkheads or not.

Some hours after the torpedoing of the tanker, our ship stopped. The convoy went past us. A corvette remained and circled us. We were told we were stopping for emergency repairs, and we watched our convoy go over the horizon. The corvette circled us for twenty-four hours. Five thousand troops sighed with relief when the screws finally started turning and the rhythmic pulse of the ship resumed.

Instead of going to Scotland, we turned back to Argentan Naval Base in St. Johns, Newfoundland, for proper repairs.

We lived on the ship for the next seven days. The gamey troops were marched ashore and we showered twenty-four at a time in a shower room with six showerheads trickling thin streams of water. We were allowed five minutes a group.

The corvette that had circled us for twenty-four hours tied up next to us in St. Johns and some of their officers came aboard our ship.

One of those officers was Eddie Duchin, the famous piano player. He was a great morale booster for us all, because he immediately wanted to know if there was a piano aboard. There was, a beat-up player piano in one of the halls, and Duchin sat down and played away on it for well over an hour.

Duchin went on and on with all the favorite tunes of the day, and then a buddy of mine, Vernon Sorensen, did a solo of "Carry Me Back to Ol' Virginny." God knows why, but even that wasn't all bad with Eddie Duchin's accompaniment.

Finally Duchin returned to the corvette, amid the wild cheers and applause of his audience.

After complete repairs we joined another convoy and successfully completed our grimey odyssey a month after leaving New York City. Arriving in Greenoch, Scotland, we embarked by train for the south of England immediately. In a meadow on the Salisbury plains near Tidworth, we pitched our pup tents. Then our officers marched us all day every day past other meadows covered with tanks and pup tents.

No one got passes, so we spent the evenings playing baseball, soccer or volleyball and waterproofing the vehicles for the coming invasion of Europe.

One evening, playing volleyball, I swung and hit a guy named Cardenelli in the head. My fingers were extended in a slap position, so my hand bent completely back and four bones snapped like twigs. My hand ballooned and I was in pain, so they sent me to the Tidworth Hospital. I ended up with my hand in a cast and was sent to the Litchfield Barracks near Coventry until the bones healed. While I was there the invasion of Europe took place.

A couple of days after D-Day, all the non-combat cripples like me were told to fall in—casualties suffering from advanced acne, volleyball injuries, or swollen goiters, and a few young paratroopers who had been in Normandy, suffered light wounds and had been evacuated back to England. They piled this mob of tattered bandaids into trucks. We didn't know where we were going. I never knew where I was going in the Army. I always had the feeling, in one of those Army trucks along with twenty or thirty other troops, like a sheep. A few times I even went "Baaa-baaa" which strangely enough made me feel better.

We joggled around in the back of this truck for about twenty minutes and arrived in the city of Birmingham. They lined us up, one column on the right side of the street, another column on the left side. My column right faced and forward marched. Although I still didn't know what the hell was going on, it was a natural condition for me in the Army, so I didn't sweat it.

"Lef', righ', lef', hup, hup, hup, tu, thee fo'."

From somewhere, the sound of a military band blended with the cadence of our marching feet. Being an old Lindy-hopper from Brooklyn, the sound of music always worked miracles with me in the service: it transformed me from a shifty-eyed, shambling yard-bird, to an eyes-straight-ahead, chest out, purposely gaited soljer, man—soljer!

The music got louder, our left feet hit Bam! on the big drum beat and crowds started to appear on the sidewalks. The cobble-stoned street went slightly uphill and curved to the left.

When a big voice boomed out, "And here are the fighting men, who just yesterday were in Normandy!," I almost fell on my ass. Christ, I felt like a fraud! My military gait dissolved to its usual shuffle and my shifty eyes darted right and left, looking for an escape. People broke from the crowd, clutched my moldy fatigue jacket and blubbered, "God bless you, Yank!" I tried to tell them with my eyes that I was an imposter. Most of all, I tried to hide the cast on my hand, but I couldn't get it in my pocket.

I slunk past the reviewing stand. Some blocks past the beribboned officers and sashed English dignitaries, the ordeal ended and we piled into the Army trucks and rode back to reality. I later found out that some sharp English PR type had come up with the inspiration to stage that fraud to hustle the

English into buying more war bonds.

My hand healed and I was re-assigned to the Infantry. I was sent to a repple depple or replacement depot at Pheasy Farms, not far from Litchfield. A replacement depot is a pool of men armies draw on to replace their casualties.

From there, I went as a replacement to Normandy about three weeks after D-Day. We disembarked on Utah Beach and marched up the sandy rise where so much desperate fighting had taken place on D-Day. About a mile in, we dug holes around the hedgerows to stay in.

There were many apple orchards, and lots of Calvados, a fiery apple brandy that was in the homes of the farmers, which quickly made its way into the hands of the soldiers. At night we'd watch the fireworks from our holes. On our left was Caen, where the English were fighting, and to our right was St. Lo, where the Americans were pushing further inland.

When I got to Normandy, I looked around for my old buddies. I finally tracked down the segment of the 999th Signal Corps with which I was supposed to have come to France. There they were, looking like so many prairie dogs in their holes: Sorensen, Glose, Woody, the whole moldy lot. It was so good to see them again, even for just a brief visit. For I was no longer part of my original outfit. I had more pressing business, like following Patton and digging all those holes so historians could follow his spoor.

As a replacement you were supposed to dig a hole, stay a day or two or three, move, dig another hole, stay awhile and move on. Your only food was K-rations, because a replacement was expected to stay only a few days until he was moved up to a combat outfit.

Not me. I stayed and stayed. I finally went to the sergeant to find out when I was going to an outfit.

"What's your name?"

"Fischetti."

The sergeant riffled through his papers and told me, "You can't go to an outfit because of your eyes—you're stamped 'non-combat.'"

"Then what am I supposed to do?" I asked.

"Jus' keep doin' what y' bin' doin'."

"I've been digging holes since Normandy and eating cruddy K-rations, an' I'm starving to death."

"Tough shit."

I went back to my hole until we moved out—again.

The American Army broke through St. Lo, and Fischetti, the taillight on this military machine, a part of but apart from, went along. St. Lo by then was only mountains of white powder that had once been buildings. Bulldozers had scraped passageways through the debris for the supply and replacement trucks to use. Knocked-out tanks, burning trucks, smoldering houses, dead cows in the fields. Dead soldiers, American and German. It was like following a maniacal giant who had gone berserk.

After St. Lo, we went south and slightly west to Avranches, then wheeled east toward Paris. I wound up in Étampes, about thirty kilometers south of Paris, which was liberated shortly thereafter.

At that point, I reviewed my inglorious military career. Two years in the States going from camp to camp, while they tried to make a radio operator out of me. I had achieved the classification but not the skill . . . the insufferable ocean voyage . . . breaking my hand playing volleyball . . . digging holes from Normandy to Étampes . . . the possibility of digging holes all the way to Berlin. I decided to go AWOL to Paris and see if I could get on *Stars and Stripes* as an artist-correspondent.

In Paris, I looked up a family I had known there before the war. Mama and Papa Legris had a daughter Simone Legris (believe it or not), who had since married a man named Boisset. I went to the Legris apartment in Paris and knocked on the door.

"Qui est la?"

"Jean."

"Jean, qui?"

"Jean Fee-shet-ee."

"Jean Fee-shet-ee!! Ooh la la!"

Mama threw the door open and wildly embraced me—"Jean!" (Le grand phoney liberateur avec gun and helmet.)

Papa was some kind of a conductor on a train, whose only English was "Zinn-zinn-a-tee." I gathered it was Cincinnati, but I never did find out why he always said it.

I explained to the Legris that I was 'sans permission,' AWOL from Étampes, and that I was seeking constructive employment in Paris. They didn't really care.

Nosing around Paris, I found out that *Stars and*

Stripes was located at the Paris *Herald Tribune* Building, 21 rue de Berri, a few blocks away from the Arc d' Triomphe.

Arriving at the *Stars and Stripes* office, I explained my ditch-digging plight and asked them if they could use an artist whose last job had been on the *Chicago Sun.* They could. They determined where I was now stationed and said they would cut orders for my transfer.

I returned to Étampes, where I hadn't even been missed, and waited. Almost a week went by, and rumors began to go around that we were going to hit the hole-digging trail again. Just as I was losing hope, a *Stars and Stripes* jeep came down the road, turned on two wheels, and a guy jumped out dramatically. He was wearing an overseas cap with a '*Stars and Stripes* Correspondent' patch on his left sleeve at the shoulder, a German parachute silk scarf, and highly polished paratrooper boots. Taking his pipe out of his mouth, he asked for the Commanding Officer and asked him if Fischetti was here.

Since officers never knew what rank, if any, *Stars and Stripes* personnel had, they usually played it safe and addressed Army newsmen as "Sir."

My C.O., a second lieutenant, was as dazzled by this guy and his jeep as we all were. He read the orders the correspondent handed him and shouted for me. I grabbed my duffle bag, gun, and helmet, and lurched over toward the two men. My lieutenant signed the transfer and motioned me to the jeep. His parting salute dissolved into a kind of "'bye, 'bye" wave. Jesus, I thought, I don't have to dig any more holes, as my rescuer gunned the jeep and roared off toward Paris.

I kept stealing sidelong glances at him during the trip, half expecting him and the jeep to disappear suddenly. He didn't, and I later found out he was something like a copyboy and not a correspondent at all.

I wound up illustrating stories, doing cartoons, and later a crummy comic strip. But covering stories for *Stars and Stripes* gave me many incredibly powerful experiences that I will never forget. It was an entirely different war for me after I arrived in Paris.

One of the benefits of working on the paper was the opportunity to meet the guys I did. One day six months after I started I went to the airport to pick up a couple of guys who were being transferred from the London edition of *Stars and Stripes* to the Paris edition. The guys I picked up were Vic Lasky and Pete Lisagor.

I was living in a huge apartment at the time with seven or eight men from *Stars and Stripes.* The apartment was available for American Army personnel because the French had arrested the previous tenants for collaborating with the Germans. Lisagor and Lasky bedded down there, too, since the place was honeycombed with rooms and men were continuously in and out as they went off on assignments.

Lisagor became the Editor of *Warweek,* a feature section of *Stars and Stripes.* Under Peter, I began to cover the stories that made such an impact on me. I covered the Petain trail in Paris, then later went to Brittany to do a story about the abortive German maneuvers that had gone on there in preparation for a German invasion of England.

To cover that story, I went to sea with a group of fishermen, four to a boat. They told me that under the Germans they had had to load their small vessels with about forty or fifty fully equipped troops, go out into the English Channel and sail back toward France. The Germans were trying to simulate an invasion of England and they used every French vessel they could lay their hands on to do it.

The fishermen said it had been a fiasco. Boats had capsized and the heavily laden German troops had gone down like rocks. Some shucked their gear but many drowned. The fishermen said you could walk to shore on the bodies.

I made sketches at sea and ashore and went back to Paris.

Later I went to Wiesbaden, Germany, to sketch a trial where six Germans, two of them women, were accused of murdering fifty thousand Germans and five thousand Russian and Polish slave laborers. The accused were being tried by the U. S. military for the murders of the five thousand Poles and Russians but not the murdered Germans.

It seemed these people had run a small hospital during the heavy Allied bombardments of Frankfurt. In the city, people had begun to run short of food and shelter, so the Frankfurt authorities trucked some people out to this hospital, ostensibly for shots against sickness; they were told they would then be sheltered and fed.

But when the unfortunates, men, women and children, arrived at this hospital, they received shots containing poison. Their bodies were stacked in the cellar until the grave digger, one of the accused, buried them.

I interviewed and sketched all of the defendants in their cells. The "spritzer," the one who actually gave the injections, was a small, meek man who cried when I asked how he could do that to human beings. He mumbled something about guaranteeing his wife and children enough to eat during the war by doing what he was told to do. He said he

The real revelations came when I went to Germany with two *Stars and Stripes* correspondents, Ed Wilcox and Alan Morrison, in the spring of 1945. Coming through the Black Forest, as far as the eye could see, we met German prisoners of war, marching west, eight abreast. The thousands of booted feet made an awesome sound, even in defeat. I thought of how chilling it must have been when these were arrogant, victorious feet, clomping down the streets of conquered cities.

We went on to Nuremberg where we saw the vast wrecked stadium, the shattered eagle, and the broken swastika on the podium from which Hitler had hypnotized crowds. The newsreels had shown the panoply of might and the roars from the throats of seemingly invincible jackbooted Nazi troops, but it had all been reduced to shambles, empty and ghostly.

We passed through countless villages and towns where white sheeting flapped desolately from windows. We were on our way to Munich, where some fighting was still going on.

Along the route we stopped at Dachau, the concentration camp which the Americans had just liberated. We parked our jeep next to a long line of freight cars filled with corpses. Moving into the camp, we passed a rectangular compound of dog houses with runs ringing them. The Americans had

knew it was terribly wrong and that he should be executed. He was. He and two others were hanged and the rest were sentenced to very long prison terms. When the Provost Marshal invited me to the hanging, I declined.

killed the Doberman pinschers and German police dogs inside, which lay where they had been destroyed. Later we found out that the brutes running the camp had had great sport by turning the vicious dogs on selected camp prisoners.

In a barracks a little further on, it was obvious that the former inhabitants had left in a great hurry. Near one of the beds was an artificial leg. We wondered where the owner was. Then about two hundred feet further down, we found six SS troops sprawled, dead, with parts of their bodies torn up. The surviving inmates said the men had been caught by the prisoners and killed, although how the prisoners managed anything like that in their condition was almost unbelievable.

One of the Nazi dead had one good leg and one stump. Presumably it was he who had left his artificial leg behind. He must have made an incredibly desperate flight, trying to keep up with his fleeing, two-legged comrades, before they were all caught by the mob of frenzied prisoners.

Next my friends and I came to a long building, sort of a warehouse. Stacked outside were great piles of shoes and clothing. Turning a corner, we came upon stacks of bodies, about eight feet high and half a city block long. Emaciated, broken-boned, naked. Their shrunken faces mirrored the terrible agonies they had endured. Not even death

had erased the evidence of torment from their faces. To the right of this obscenity were the ovens in which the Germans burned the inmates. Some of the charred bodies were still there. The stench was incredible.

American soldiers were standing around. They had rounded up many of the inhabitants of the small town of Dachau to press them into service burying the bodies. The townspeople tried to shut out the sight, turning their heads or burying their faces in their hands. The people of Dachau said they had had no idea of this.

I shut my eyes and pinched my arm, hard. I thought I must be dreaming this nightmare. But when I opened my eyes it was all there. The sight will never leave me.

For a year afterward, I had the same recurring nightmare. Camp prisoners would float toward me, skeleton figures, wearing tattered, striped clothing. Then the skull in the foreground would get closer and closer, open his mouth, and the wail of a siren would begin to sound. I'd wake up again and again, shaken and wet.

At the main gate of the camp we entered the building that guarded the gate. It was a shambles. Papers, furniture, cabinets strewn about. I pocketed the large key to the main gate from the key board. When I returned to Paris I gave it to a Frenchman, a friend of mine, a Jew, as a sort of symbol that the horror was over. In return, he gave me his yellow patch with the Star of David and "*Juif*" or "Jew" inside the Star. I brought it home and put it in my Bible.

Wilcox, Morrison and I left Dachau to head for Munich. Just inside the city we decided to bang on the door of one of the houses we were passing and ask for something to eat.

Alan Morrison was elected, so he went up and knocked. The door opened cautiously. A woman appeared who seemed terrified at seeing Alan. Ed Wilcox spoke some German and so he assured her that all we wanted was something to eat. She allowed us inside, and her husband helped her get something for us. On a bureau in the living room we saw a picture of a blond, twenty-ish youth in an SS uniform. The woman told us her son had written terrifying letters back home about the black Moorish troops his outfit had faced in Italy.

He had told how for sport the blacks crept into German foxholes, killed one of its two inhabitants without waking the other, then cut off the ears of the dead one, pocketing them as souvenirs and returning to their lines. To say that this would demoralize the survivor is putting it mildly. I would have been a basket case.

This boy's mother, who had never seen a black, saw our Alan, who was a black, and was understandably terrified.

While we were eating, there was a knock on the door. A British soldier entered, laden with food for this German couple. Angry, we asked the Englishman why the hell he was feeding Germans while the war was still going on. He told us that when he was shot down two years before and was a prisoner, he was assigned to clearing up rubble in the streets. These two Germans at great risk to themselves had slipped food to him whenever they could. The British airman said these weren't German traitors, they were just ordinary people who had felt for him.

After eating we thanked the couple and drove away. We saw no Germans, civilian or military, just American soldiers. There was no noise, just occasional shots, now and then. When we pulled up in front of the City Hall in Munich, only a colonel, a sergeant and a private were there. No one else. The colonel told us that the war was over in Europe.

He passed a bottle of whiskey around. That was it, no whooping, hollering, nothing. Just the war was over. We headed back to Paris.

NEW YORK

I was shipped back from the Army through one of the "cigarette camps" (named Camel, Chesterfield, Lucky Strike, etc.) around Marseilles, and arrived back in New York during the first week in January, 1946.

I ran into my old friend Lenny Karsakov, who'd been a senior at Pratt when we were all freshmen. He'd been in the OSS during the war, but had no more plans now than I, so we got an apartment together on West 100th Street, a five-flight walk-up, just off Riverside Drive. We couldn't afford a phone for a long time, so we always kept our door open to hear the telephone five flights down in the lobby. As free-lancers, it was the umbilical cord that sustained us. For every twenty wild dashes down the five flights to answer the phone, one was for us.

I guess I did everything in the line of free-lancing to survive until I could get a shot at doing what I wanted to do, political cartoons. I drew gags, ads, juvenile books, university magazine illustrations, drawings on babies' bibs, towels, pamphlets, throwaways. I was doing spots for *Pageant* magazine, the *New York Times Magazine* section, *Coronet,* and lots of little jobs here and there in small studios as well. All of them paid, some right away, others in a month or two.

I only came close to being screwed financially once. A fly-by-night outfit assigned me to do quite a few illustrations. Then they delayed paying me for a couple of months. I started to dun them. Time went on. No action. As the same silence continued for the next two or three months, I got madder and madder. I don't like being screwed. I warned them that if my money wasn't there the next time I came down, I was going to chuck things out the window—typewriters, file cabinets, chairs, whatever—until it added up to what they owed me. I really didn't give a damn if I went to jail. They were wrong to have had me do work and not have paid me for it, and it made me furious to have been taken.

The following week, when I went in to collect, there was no check. I stormed into a room, grabbed a typewriter and went to the window. People started to fly all around and someone told me not to do anything rash, that I'd be paid. I stayed near the window suspecting they'd call the cops. They didn't. A guy came in with a check for the full amount. I put the typewriter down and left. They were the only potential deadbeats I've ever run into in thirty-five years of "writin' them pictures," as a boyhood Brooklyn friend describes what I do.

Anyway, Lenny finally met a nice Jewish girl from the Bronx and married her. I went to the wedding and at the temple I got a crepe paper yarmulke which kept sliding up my head until it popped straight up and off. Every time I put the yarmulke back on, the same thing happened. The people in the rows behind me were beside themselves trying to keep from disturbing the ceremony with uncontrolled laughter. Lenny the natural comedian was too busy at the time to make people laugh, but I became his surrogate, doing it, inadvertently.

After Lenny got married, Bernie Lewis, the editor who had offered me the $35 extra that time at *Esquire* in Chicago, moved into the West 100th Street apartment with me. He had been in the Office of War Information during the war, and since returning had been living with his folks out on Long Island, trying to avoid getting trapped in the family business as his father wanted. But by then he'd had it and was ready to work full-time as a writer. For the next year, he worked from six in the morning until midnight, trying to write a book about his war experiences. When he got a contract from a publisher, we all exulted, but the book never saw the light of day. Another guy from his outfit had the same idea, and got his book published first. At the end of a year, Bernie left to marry the girl he'd been going with.

That ended an era. By the time Bernie moved out, I had a fairly healthy free-lance business going, so I took the opportunity to move to a much better apartment on West 44th Street. At this point, I lived a real bachelor's existence: nothing but a six-pack of beer in the refrigerator at any one time, and exactly one suit hanging in the large walk-in closet. It was used only to deliver finished jobs.

Life continued like that for some time. By then, I was 32 and enjoying what seemed to me the good life.

Then in 1948, at the birthday party given for Al Avison's Danish actress friend, I met Karen and within six weeks we were married. Before we were married she briefed me on this tiny Valhalla, which she said contained four million Danes. What she didn't tell me was that that was *inside* the country.

We've been married twenty-five years, and I swear there have been at least twice the four million Danes she mentioned trooping through our living room.

Karen, a stewardess with the Scandinavian Airline System (SAS) also told me about her family. Her Mom and Dad had been in the hotel and restaurant business in various towns in Jutland, Denmark. She was their only child.

Her father loved to sing and at one time considered making it his profession. I never met him, but Karen had great rapport with him and describes him as a spirited man of great humor who loved belting out the songs in church. In his middle forties he became ill and was bed-ridden; he then died in his middle fifties.

The family was always strapped for money because of Karen's father's illnesses and the failures of the various hotel enterprises. Through it all, Karen's mother, Kristina, was a tower of strength. She had come from a farm where hardship was a part of her very large family. Kristina was always there to help her brothers and sisters and the many, many relatives, but she always resented her parents bringing into the world so many more children than they could support.

The Danes from Jutland are very much like our New Englanders, somewhat dour, taciturn and not what you would call heavy tippers. I first really understood this the first time I met my mother-in-law. It was twenty-five years ago at a railroad station in Copenhagen. She was getting off a train from the last leg of her journey from Jutland. So we wouldn't miss her, Karen had devised a plan whereby she would wait at the end of the platform and I would go to the train to look for a woman I had never seen.

Thanks to Karen's superb description of her mother and my keen Neapolitan eye, I zeroed in on a little woman with a certain kind of a hat, carrying a satchel.

"Mor?" I questioned, grabbing the handle of the satchel.

The little woman grabbed her satchel back. Jutlanders don't trust many people, especially satchel grabbers in railroad stations.

I kept saying "Mor" and yanking on the satchel handle, and she kept yanking it toward her. Finally, after see-sawing back and forth for some time, she looked at me and said,

"Yonny?"

I smiled and said, "Yeah, Yonny," and we went on to meet Karen.

Despite this forbidding build-up, I found that the Danes are quite a happy, fun-loving people. They have a song for every occasion. Mention a wildflower swaying in a breeze—there's a song about it. Mention rice being thrown at a bride—there's a song about it. Danes love people, parties and pricking pompous idiots. Their love for each other is almost as great as it is for visitors to their land.

In departing at a railroad station, an airport or a ship's dock, the family and friends are there to see you off, many with small Danish flags. The red and white national flags are often used at dinner tables, and at Christmastime strings of tiny paper Danish flags decorate the Christmas tree in between the ornaments and lighted candles.

Karen has all of the traditional Danish virtues. She's a great cook and like so many Danish women I know takes a lot of time preparing colorful and appetizing tables for her guests. Danes revel in the whole procedure of preparing for and entertaining their guests and they also enjoy their own parties very much.

Karen and I lived happily and well in the apartment on West 44th Street for about a year. By then Karen was pregnant, and we began to look for the proverbial house in the country in which to raise kids. In 1950 we finally found a very modest little place that looked like a Kraft cheese box, in a back woods area of Cos Cob, Connecticut. Because of the thick woods and the remoteness of the location, no one had wanted it. However, the very week that we saw it, a wealthy doctor looking for a weekend home decided he had to have it, and offered the owner $1,500 more than the asking price. Fortunately, the owner was more concerned that her elderly father who lived next door have full-time, companionable neighbors than she was about money, and she let us have the place for the lower price and almost no down payment.

Back in the city, we prepared to move, but first we stopped for the arrival of our son, Peter. One sunny afternoon, Karen and I had lunch in a basement French café opposite the Barbizon Hotel for Women, then casually walked over to St. Clare's Hospital on the West Side, where Peter was delivered, and we were more or less ready to begin life as a family in Connecticut. We lived in Cos Cob for eighteen years, although one of our trips into the city two years later was to return to St. Clare's so that the same doctor who had delivered Peter could deliver our second son. Michael was named after that doctor.

Michael was only five pounds when he was born, and then he lost weight. He had to stay in the hospital after Karen left until he was five pounds again.

Mor made her first visit to America then, to help care for Michael. She was sixty-three.

Mor stayed with us for a year and half. She took great care of Michael and fed her frail grandson constantly. She elected to stay until he started walking, a year and a half later. It's wonderful to see now that at 6 feet 3 inches he towers over his tiny grandmother, although he is still thin. And she still has a special smile in her eyes when she looks at him.

By now, we've been to Denmark above five times in all, and Mor has visited us five or six times.

On a couple of the trips to Denmark we rented a car and drove Mor, who now lives in Silkeborg, all over Jutland, to the North Sea, with its windy, sandy beaches, and the tumbling, grotesque German pill-boxes which slide down the steep embankments toward the beach.

I asked why they didn't destroy these ugly reminders of the Nazi occupation, and I was told that the reinforced concrete, many feet thick, seems impervious to dynamite. When the Danes tried blasting them, windows and foundations of the houses in nearby Lokken were shaken and damaged.

There were never many cars on the road and so we could just admire the incredible scenery: gentle rolling hills, every inch under cultivation, different colored rectangular fields of wheat, barley and oats. Along the sides of the roads were poppies, cornflowers and daisies.

When I remarked to Karen and Mor that they had a beautiful land, they told me that their national anthem is, "There Is A Beautiful Country."

After we moved to Connecticut, I often commuted into the city, because in 1951 I went to work for the Newspaper Enterprise Association (NEA) where I stayed for ten years. I shared an office there with Bruce Biossat for eight years. Now the Washington Bureau Chief for NEA, then he wrote editorials, while I drew political cartoons.

Politics is a passion with Bruce, who'll cover *any* political event, even a race for dog-catcher, and love it.

Accurate figures are also a passion with him. I've never seen *anyone* come as close as he does on delegate counts at national political conventions. I'm sure when Bruce goes to heaven he'll know within one or two how many are there.

Jimmy Breslin and I also worked together at NEA. He was an assistant sports editor then. Once, Jimmy shuffled into the office Bruce and I shared, stocky body topped by a mass of blue-black hair and asked,

"Y' ever win th' Pulitzer, John?"

"No."

"Y' wanna win it?"

"Sure I do."

"Tell y' what. Go get two grand from the front office f' me."

"What the hell for? . . . "

"One grand walkin' aroun' dough f' me aroun' Columbia University and the other gran' for one a them hungry professors . . . "

"Christ, Jimmy, who the hell wants a Pulitzer *that* way?!!!"

"Whatta y' mean *that* way?"

Another time when I was standing in the Sports Department talking to Jimmy, I happened to say, just as Harry Grayson, the Sports Editor, was walking by, "Jesus, Jimmy, you're a cynic." Grayson overheard this, took the cigar out of his mouth, looked at me and said, "Cynic?!! . . . Why, that son of a bitch thought World War II was fixed."

After having lived in Chicago for six years and seeing pol after pol go down the drain, while others die before going down the drain but leave loads of loot all over, Jimmy's cynical observation about World War II doesn't seem nearly as outrageous now as it did in the 50's.

I saw Jimmy during the Democratic Convention in Miami in '72. He was a delegate in the New York contingent and my wife Karen and I went to his room. I told Breslin I was writing this book and asked if he'd mind if I told a couple of stories about him that weren't particularly flattering.

"Nah! Go ahead, an' if y' can't think 'a some real good ones, make some up."

With Breslin, who needs to make them up?

Those were the good parts of NEA. What wasn't so great was that the regimen there was to work on ideas and submit four or five roughs each day to your editor. NEA is, or at least was, a service when I worked for them—I don't know if they have the same setup now.

With a service, you receive a flat salary for your work; a syndicate splits 50-50 with the cartoonist on all money that accrues from sales of your cartoons to as many newspapers as will buy them. The sale price is determined by the circulation of the paper, how much in demand a cartoonist is, or how good the salesman is at *his* work. When you're syndicated, you sink or swim on your own. No sales, you take a fall.

In a service, you're part of a package that includes comic strips, editorials, sports, fashions, columns—just about everything that makes up a newspaper. The service sells the complete package to newspapers all over the country.

So, when you're doing political cartoons for a service and you happen to piss off an editor in Curmudgeon, Georgia, he can threaten to cut off the *whole* package, if that so and so Fischetti keeps on disagreeing with him. My editor at NEA, Boyd Lewis, was really great at bringing fiery client temperatures down and he made my stay there tolerable. I did do some good things there and Boyd worked like hell to smooth things out with clients, but I kept feeling that I would be a much better cartoonist if I had complete freedom.

So in the second year of one of my three-year contracts I told Boyd that I planned to quit at the end of my contract and that he should start looking for a new cartoonist. I had been with NEA for ten years by then. I was forty-four years old.

Very exciting things were happening then at the *Herald Tribune,* and I thought that maybe they would be interested in a cartoonist who wanted complete freedom.

John Hay Whitney, United States Ambassador to the Court of St. James, had purchased the *New York Herald Tribune* from the Reid family about five years before and had hired John Denson, former editor of *Newsweek,* as editor of the *Herald Tribune.*

I showed my stuff to Denson who was very interested and said he'd speak to Whitney about my demands for editorial freedom, salary, working at home, etc.

About a month later he called me and we made a date to have lunch with his assistant, Bob Albert, and the *New York Herald Tribune* Syndicate Manager, Lloyd Hagen. We all had a very pleasant lunch and then got down to business. Denson told me that Jock Whitney had liked my work very much and told him to sign me to a one-year contract giving me everything I had asked for. No chiseling, cutting back, dickering—no chicken shit—I was just to do my cartoons the way I wanted to do them.

Denson then asked me if they could syndicate my work. I had been so preoccupied with getting my freedom that the thought of syndication simply had not occurred to me. At NEA I had been in over 800 papers, and all that so many papers had come to mean to me was complaining editors and trouble. So, offhandedly, I agreed to let them syndicate me. I was so damned happy about doing my thing and being on the *Trib,* I couldn't have cared less about anything else. When we finished lunch, John Denson got up, embraced me and told me how happy he was.

He was happy! . . . I ran down the stairs and down 34th Street to a phone booth in the Port Authority Building to tell my wife Karen that they had given me everything I had wanted—and so delightfully!

For about four years before joining the *Trib*, I had been dumping gag ideas in a drawer. I just couldn't help thinking them up and jotting them down. I had no plans to do anything with them. I had done the gag magazine rounds for a while after the Army and had found it rather demeaning to run around every Wednesday to the cartoon editors of all the magazines and wait for word from them that they wanted finishes on the roughs they had selected. It also entailed a lot of bookkeeping, and continually sending the roughs that were turned down to the smaller, cheaper magazines.

I never did get out of the habit of jotting ideas down, but I just threw them in a drawer. One day, my wife Karen saw them and commented that it was a pity I didn't do something with them. I thought so too. We had subscribed to *Punch* Magazine which is published in London for some time and since I had always admired the English cartoonists, I decided to beard the Englishman in his den and see if I could compete successfully with him. Out of the first batch I sent to *Punch,* they bought two. Then they welcomed me to *Punch* and asked if I would continue contributing. I did, and sold cartoons to them for three years. Compared with American standards, the pay was lousy, but spiritually I was a millionaire!

Before starting at the *Trib,* I decided to change my format and my technique. I went to a shallow, wider rectangle, ditched my grease crayon and worked with brush and pen. I began to use a gray dotted paper which was called Ben-Day then (Zip–a–Tone now) for the grays in my cartoons. I decided to weld my line drawings from *Punch* together with my American political cartooning technique.

Just two months after going with the *Trib* in 1961, the syndicate informed me that I was to appear in seventy-five papers. Since then, the cancellations and the new papers have run about even so I'm in about the same number of papers now as I was then.

Since syndication wasn't included in my original plans, the fact that so many papers wanted to buy my cartoons added exhilaration to the great satisfaction of the freedom I now enjoyed doing my work.

I decided to do my work at home because I didn't

"*I feel awful.*"

want *anyone* to have an opportunity to lean on me in *any* way. I figured if I wasn't around anyone no one would have an opportunity to "suggest" this or that. I was determined to prove that I was a far better cartoonist than I had shown heretofore.

Working alone, one has to rely on one's own judgment as to what's good or bad. With some cartoons it's easy. You know it immediately. Everything's just right with the idea. The picture is composed in your mind and you can hardly wait to do the actual drawing.

With some ideas you *think* you have something, but the certainty is missing. Then you have to labor and hone and hone the idea until you know it's one you won't be ashamed of.

Working at home, the only person you can bounce ideas off is your wife. That of course leads to many extra cat fights that you could have avoided by being in town fighting with your editor. But fighting at home has a slight advantage: my wife is prettier than any editor I've ever known.

I did miss the contact of fellow newspapermen, the small and large talk that triggers a thought process. So I went to the *Herald Tribune* from time to time to talk to friends, or to attend editorial conferences which I had been invited to attend any time I wanted by Whitney and Dwight Sargent, Editor of the editorial page. Sometimes I just went to have lunch or enjoy the cocktail hour at Bleecks (formerly the Artist and Writers Club) from five until whenever.

But I always found the editorial conferences that I did attend at the *Herald Tribune* very informative. Besides Sargent, the Editor of the editorial page, the other editorial page staff members were Harry Baehr, Ray Price, L. L. Engelking, Herb Kupferberg, and Dan Dowling, the cartoonist. I learned a lot from the specialists in each field even though I didn't always agree with their stands.

But one day I stormed into Denson, the editor's, office, to bitch about the size of one of my cartoons, which had appeared in the letters column about the size of an air mail stamp. Denson called Sargent, really chewed him out, then suggested to Sargent that he get to know me. I was taken to Dwight's office for the introduction, and I wasn't very impressed. Here was this neat man, tie just so, black suit, highly polished shoes. I thought he was one of the squarest guys I had ever seen. We mumbled something to each other and left it at that.

Some days later Sargent called my home and invited me to lunch. It was a little embarrassing sitting across from him. But we both ordered martinis, and I knew then that this guy couldn't be *all* bad. We had a few more, then lunch. He told me what he was all about and he laughed about the chewing-out Denson had given him.

Dwight just looks square. Scratch those highly polished shoes and out pops a man who loves people, life and laughter. He's been a dear friend of mine for years now. Dwight left the *Trib* to become the curator of the Neiman Program at Harvard. He recently resigned that job and is now President of the National Freedom of Information Foundation at the School of Journalism of the University of Missouri.

I also learned something at one of the monthly meetings of the National Cartoonists Society I attended some time after I had gone with the *Trib.* A political cartoonist friend of mine, in town for this particular meeting, complimented me on the improvement in my work and wanted to know the details of the change. What most impressed him was that I didn't have to submit roughs and get okays from anyone to go ahead with the finish. He declared that he was going to demand that of his editor when he returned home.

Three or four months later, I ran into him again at another National Cartoonists Society meeting. He told me that after our last talk he had confronted his editor and demanded to work the way I worked. He had demanded to be unleashed. Without batting an eye, his editor pronounced him unleashed. My friend said that he had worked without his editor for about a week to ten days, and then asked his editor if they could resume their former method of operating.

So my friend threw in the freedom sponge and continued happily working with his editor. When I asked him why, his reply was that he just couldn't decide on his own whether an idea was any good or not. He's a damned fine cartoonist and obviously his editor was a good one who wasn't trying to restrain him in any way but just wanted a good cartoon.

I work best unhampered, my friend doesn't. The point is for us all to produce our best cartoons, however we do it.

I stayed at the *Herald Tribune* until the paper folded in 1966. But the *Herald Tribune* lives, in Paris. It's called the *International Herald Tribune* now and its Editor is Murray M. Weiss, known as "Buddy" Weiss to almost everyone. Buddy is the former City Editor of the New York *Herald Tribune,* and a former *New York Times* man a couple of times.

It's amazing how proud one can be of working on a newspaper. To me, the *Herald Tribune* is Mrs. Reid, John Denson, Geoffrey Parsons, Sr., Dick Schaap, Jim Bellows, Jimmy Breslin, Red Smith, Stanley Woodward, Dave Murray, Everett Walker, Maggie Higgins, Homer Bigart, Luke Carroll, Roger

"OH, COUP D'ETATS ARE GREAT FOR <u>YOU</u> — YOU'RE OUT MEETING INTERESTING PEOPLE WHILE <u>I</u> STAY HOME ALONE BOARDING UP THE WINDOWS"

Kahn, Judith Crist, Belle Rosenbaum, Irita Van Doren, Dick Wald, Jock Whitney, Herb Kupferberg, Lawton Carver, Ben Price, Dan Dowling, Ding, Warren Rogers, Bob Donovan, Earl Mazo, Tom O'Hara, Clay Felker, Betsy and George Bates, Don Cook, Bill Mauldin, David Wise, Al Von Entress . . .

The *Trib* was a very special paper that attracted great talent throughout the many years that it lived. Today, just seeing the masthead on the Paris *Herald Tribune* makes me feel good. I will always feel a damn sight better just to know that it's healthy, making money, and in the hands of men who care very much not just about publishing a paper, but the *Herald Tribune* in particular.

By the time I was at the *Trib* my ex-roommate, Lenny Karsakov, had become the art director of an advertising agency in Boston, and since it was such a short trip between Connecticut and Massachusetts, his family and mine remained very close. They are my son Peter's godparents. Imagine that, a Jewish godfather! *Oi vey!*

Their three daughters, Joan, Ellie, and Jill, are like our own. They call Karen "Aunt," and me, "Uncle Johnny."

On one visit to their home in Massachusetts, Ellie, the middle girl, was sitting on my lap. She had taken a great interest in religion, and asked me how old I had been when I was bar mitzvahd.

When I told her I had never been bar mitzvahd, her jaw fell. She couldn't believe that anyone, let alone Uncle Johnny and Aunt Karen, weren't Jewish. It took some explaining to establish the fact that John Fischetti had been confirmed in a German Lutheran Church.

In Connecticut, cartoonists always played a very large role in our lives. There were many more there than there are in Chicago. We golfed, bowled, ate, swam and entertained together, and all our wives were friends.

In fact, all who've ever been in our home have been there because we've wanted them. Those friends we have who do entertain for business reasons more often than not have to put up with bores, louts and clods. But we had good times.

John Cullen Murphy draws the strip *Big Ben Bolt* and lately has also been doing the Sunday *Prince Valiant.* He and his wife Joan are committed conservatives and some of the most delightful evenings we've spent were talking politics, needling and being needled by them. Also among our circle in Connecticut were Curt Swan, who had been on *Stars and Stripes* with me in Paris, whose wife Helene had been a Red Cross girl there. In fact, I was their best man when they were married in Paris.

Mort Walker is the creator of *Beetle Bailey, Hi and Lois,* and *Boners' Ark.* He and Johnny Hart, who created *B. C.* and *Wizard of Id,* are two of the tycoons of the cartoon business, both bulging at the seams with assistants and long green.

Dik Browne draws *Hi and Lois* for Mort and has just come up with a strip of his own, *Hagar the Horrible,* about a Viking and his family. If, as they say, Heywood Broun looked like an unmade bed, my friend Dik Browne looks like an unmade bed with Heywood Broun sleeping in it.

His wife Joan is always at him to pull his trousers up—she claims he looks like he's melting. We, his friends, know he *has* melted and so we never nag him about pulling up his pants.

Like Heywood Broun, he's very smart, so it sort of evens things out for us to feel superior about his lack of neatness. After all, everyone knows that in winning contests, neatness counts.

Dik and Joan give parties for which they should charge rent—people hang in there for days. I know—Karen and I were the last ones out a few times.

Bud Jones, Jerry Dumas and Bob Gustafson are all part of Mort Walker's funny money empire. They draw the characters and write gags for all of the strips along with Mort. They and their wives were all part of our scene in Connecticut.

In fact, my fellow cartoonists and I were all so close and so much like a team then that when I was voted one of the winners at one of the annual National Cartoonists Society award dinners, Karen was convinced that it was as much popularity as the spectacular quality of my cartoons. She looked at me ironically and said, "I didn't know that many cartoonists bowled." It's true that I haven't won any cartoon society awards since I've been in Chicago.

Not all the cartoonists I met in those years lived in the immediate vicinity, of course. But there were lots of National Cartoonists Society dinners and get-togethers, and other related professional events, so that gradually I met most if not all of my youthful heroes, and those of my peers whom I admired the most.

Rube Goldberg—comic strip cartoonist, writer, political cartoonist, Pulitzer Prize winner. The Reuben Award, the highest honor the National Cartoonists Society can bestow on one of its members was named after him. Rube Goldberg is a part of our vocabulary and Rube Goldberg is a part of every cartoonist who ever knew him.

He was in his eighties when he started to sculpt, and he was both prolific and excellent at it. He once told me that he always woke up in the morning with his head full of ideas and as excited as any young art student.

The Scepter

He had a fabulous life, a fabulous career, and was a truly fabulous man.

Milton Caniff started his successful career drawing *Terry and the Pirates.* Quite a few years ago he stopped doing that strip and created *Steven Canyon*, a strip he's still doing successfully.

As a youngster absolutely ape on newspaper cartoons, when I saw this beautifully drawn strip with China as its locale and all those great looking dames and handsome guys, I thought the millenia had arrived in cartooning.

I wrote a fan letter to Caniff about the strip, never expecting a reply. A short time later a letter arrived at my home in Brooklyn from Milton Caniff himself! It was a long beautiful letter, thanking me for my praise and encouraging me to work hard and stay at cartooning. Just hearing from him was wild but sharing intimate cartoonists' stuff like, "Stay with it!" *Nirvana* for a young would-be cartoonist.

I never forgot this and all through my professional career, I've tried to answer and help young cartoonists as Milton helped me.

Today, he's both a good friend and still my hero.

I guess Harry Devlin has to be the classiest cartoonist I've ever met. He can turn his hand to the loosest kinds of comic and straight illustration, then he can tighten up and do the most disciplined illustrations you've ever seen.

We alternated doing political cartoons in full color for *Collier's* every other or every third week. They used others whenever we didn't appear.

Harry's sense of drawing and color is just fabulous. He and his wife Wendy, a professional portrait painter and juvenile book author, used to have a whole houseful of kids in Mountainside, New Jersey.

Harry now teaches, writes and illustrates very elaborate books on architecture. His kids are all grown up now and I've sort of lost track of them all, but one never forgets or loses track of Harry Devlin's great mind and talent.

One of my heroes, though, I never really got to know. The great political cartoonist, Rollin Kirby, was the first Pulitzer Prize winner and subsequently won two more Pulitzers.

I did sort of meet him when I was an elevator operator at the Gramercy Park Hotel in New York City where he lived, but although I used to take him up and down often, of course I never let on that he was my idol or that I had any aspirations to be a cartoonist, too.

In 1951, I won the National Headliners' Medal for political cartooning. My editor, Boyd Lewis of the Newspaper Enterprise Association, knew the story about Kirby, me and the Gramercy Park Hotel, and without telling me, Boyd contacted Kirby and told him the story. He asked Kirby to present the medal to me. Kirby, touched and delighted, told Boyd he would be honored to do it.

But Rollin Kirby died a few days before the presentation. Boyd told me about it after Kirby's death. I was heartbroken.

CHICAGO

The *Herald Tribune* Syndicate had been jointly owned by Jock Whitney and Marshall Field. Field also owned the *Chicago Daily News.* So when the *Tribune* folded, Ken McArdle, an old friend from Connecticut who by then was Editor of the editorial page of the *Daily News,* told me not to accept any of the offers I was getting from around the country, but to wait and talk to Roy Fisher, then the Editor of the *Daily News.*

As it happened, shortly thereafter, I was a speaker at a Nieman Fellows seminar in Cambridge which Fisher attended, and so we met then. Barring a total personality conflict with Fisher or Marshall Field or one of the other top management people at the *Daily News,* I had already decided it was the place I'd most like to go after the *Tribune.* Many of my old cronies were working there by then.

But there was no problem with Fisher. Roy, a handsome silver-haired Kansan, is a former Nieman Fellow whose dad, like the fathers of so many newspapermen, was a minister. We had great rapport immediately and in all my years at the *Daily News,* he never bugged me, but left me free to do my work in my own way. Roy is an essentially good man and I never have trouble with that kind.

I remember his outrage when we both visited the tiny apartment of Black Panther Chairman Fred Hampton and Mark Clark, right after the two Panthers were killed and several others, including two women, were wounded in a shoot-in with State's Attorney Edward V. Hanrahan's police. Fisher and I counted over seventy bullet holes that came into the apartment from outside and saw that there were no bullet marks going out. It was a disgusting performance by the Chicago police and Roy made no attempt to keep silent about how he felt about it.

About a year later, in 1971, Roy decided to leave the frantic editor's life for academe. My wife Karen and I, on the way back from Topeka, Kansas, stopped in Columbia, Missouri, to see Roy who had then just accepted his current position as Dean of the School of Journalism at the University of Missouri. He had left his wife Anne back in Glencoe, Illinois, to take care of the kids and the hundreds of details of wrapping up a life in one place to begin again in another.

While we were there, Roy asked us if we'd mind going to a cocktail party someone was having to help him to meet friends and faculty at the university. I was standing next to my wife and Roy when a little elderly lady came up to me and gushed, "Ooh! Are you Dean Fisher?" Over my shoulder, I replied for him, "You're goddamned right I am, and there are gonna be some changes made around here." She almost swallowed her swizzle stick as I tapped Roy on the shoulder to tell him someone wanted to meet him. He got a good laugh out of it, although he'd never have said that himself.

The brass in any outfit holds the key to happiness or misery as far as a political cartoonist or any other underling is concerned. It's not a half bad group at the *Daily News.*

Marshall Field is Numero Uno. We have a nice, arms-length relationship: "Hi, John. Hi Marsh." One encounter with Field does stick out in my memory, though.

My wife had been after me for three or four years to buy a new raincoat to replace the tattered rag I was very attached to. I had beat back all of her nefarious schemes to replace my beloved with a sleek new model. She finally made an end run and I wound up with a gleaming new raincoat. So help me, on my very first day out with it, I ran into Marshall in the elevator of the newspaper building. Damn if he didn't say, "Hi, John, see you got a new raincoat."!!!

We have one other connection: I live next door to him. I always thought it's nice to know he's there if ever I want to borrow a cup of money.

John G. Trezevant as Executive Vice-President is Number One to Numero Uno. We all call him "Dick" or "Trez." The Trez I understand, but where the Dick in "John G. Trezevant" comes from has always eluded me. Before coming to Chicago, he too was on the same sinking ship, *Colliers,* that Ken McArdle and I were on. A first-class human being, he's a man who flies in the face of Lippy Durocher's scabby observation that nice guys finish last.

He has a habit of sticking gold stars on cartoons I've done that he particularly likes. The kind you were rewarded with in Sunday School for perfect attendance. Then he keeps you off balance by holding back for long periods, and coming up with one just when you're beginning to believe you've shot your wad as a cartoonist.

Bill Steven who recently went into three-quarter retirement, has also been an important part of the *Daily News* for me. One of the most avid cartoon buffs around and one hell of a newspaperman, Bill is the former Editor of the *Minneapolis Tribune,* former Editor of the *Houston Chronicle,* and the partly retired Executive Vice-President of the *Daily News.*

When I asked Ken McArdle what the hell that title meant, Ken said that was a vice-president with clout. Bill has had quite a career.

He reads newspapers like no else I've ever seen, mentally juggling everything: this story against that one, this ad could've gone here, that one there, this should have gone there. . . . He can't stop, he even does it on vacations.

He knows cartoons just as well. He's current on the story line in all the straight, serious strips, and reads and knows every comic strip or panel that exists. Up until his recent part retirement, he regularly showed up at all the National Cartoonists Society's annual dinners with his wife. Not as an editor—just as a buff.

Emmett Dedmon is Editorial Director of both the *Chicago Sun-Times* and *Chicago Daily News* and is the former Editor of the *Chicago Sun-Times.* When I won the Pulitzer, Emmett threw himself into supervising the compiling of a book of the most memorable of the hundreds of letters and messages I had received. He did the job with such zeal that I could hardly carry the book home, it was so big. And I treasure it.

It's another side of Emmett who's known as a tough bastard who isn't afraid of a fight. And he's had a lot of them.

Often when you pick up a copy of the *Chicago Journalism Review*—the magazine created by harassed and disenchanted newsmen after the 1968 Democratic Convention disorders which reports behind the scenes of the news business—they are raking Emmett over the coals for the way he handled one story or another. They always accuse him of having ulterior motives in his treatment of the news, of breakfasting with the *bête-noire* Daley all the time and of operating hand in glove with the Mayor and business interests at the expense of the ordinary man and woman in Chicago. Emmett points out that in his position he can't help having at least a nodding acquaintance with the Mayor and business leaders but he denies having or promoting special interests and fights his accusers very hard.

I suspect it's Emmett's temper and less than diplomatic way of handling people that is at the root of a lot of people's reactions toward him. I know one very mild-mannered guy whom Dedmon once chewed out in front of a whole newsroom full of reporters, who will never forgive Dedmon and swears he'll get revenge one day.

Another newsman told me of the time when he went into the newsroom and bugged Emmett about the way he was handling a story while all hell was breaking loose on the streets during the Democratic Convention. Red-faced, Emmett turned on the guy and roared out an invitation to come out right then and fight him in the alley. The journalist declined and later admitted to me that while his facts were right, his timing was probably bad.

But Emmett has never leaned on me and we get along just fine.

Daryle Feldmeir is the Editor of the *Daily News.* We came to Chicago within a month of each other, he from the *Minneapolis Tribune,* I from the New York *Trib.* Strangely enough, he spent exactly eighteen years in Minneapolis and I was eighteen years in Cos Cob.

Daryle came to the *Daily News* as Managing Editor. When he became Editor, Mike Royko gave him a book of his columns which he inscribed. He put "To____" and wrote out the names of the long line of former short-lived editors, whose names he scratched out. The last line was, "To Daryle Feldmeir." Mike followed it with, "Good luck. Mike."

A WEEK IN THE LIFE OF MAYOR RICHARD J. DALEY

Daryle attends almost all of the editorial conferences and the comments he makes are usually quite pungent. At one meeting he remarked on the caliber of people running for public office in Chicago as compared to those running for office in Minneapolis. He pointed out that in Minneapolis your problem most often was to decide between two great aspirants, and it was difficult because both were so good. In Chicago, he commented, it was difficult because both were so bad, you had to pick the one that was less bad.

Daryle is unflappable, and in a crisis he will tell a joke, which in no way detracts from his serious, deep concern for his fellow man and the world he lives in. But he *is* a smart-ass.

This is the first book I've ever written, and because of it, I became curious about other newspapermen's forays into the book world.

To my surprise, I found that many journalists who write every day have never written a book. Daryle also answered negatively when asked if he had ever written a book. When I asked him why not, he replied, "I *know* when I have nothing to say."

Ken McArdle is and was when I began, the Editor of the editorial page on the *Chicago Daily News.* I had met Ken when I was working for NEA and moonlighted political cartoons for *Colliers'* magazine for about five years. During the last few years of *Colliers'* life, Ken was the Editor and I did one or two cartoons a month in living color for him. Also, Ken lived in New Canaan, Connecticut, which is very near Cos Cob, and so we became good friends. Like so many others who know Ken, I trust him implicitly and consider him incapable of doing anything mean to gain an advantage. In addition, he's an excellent editorial writer and editor.

According to the terms of the contract I signed with the *Daily News,* I would not have to clear my work with anyone. I could just do my cartoon and hand it in, as I had on the New York *Herald Tribune.* When I had gotten to the *Herald Tribune,* I had wanted no part of censoring because of my NEA experience; so I had worked at home and brought my finished work to the paper.

But having worked this way for some years, I gained confidence and was not as jumpy about people trying to emasculate my cartoons when I came to the *Chicago Daily News.* Ken and I understood each other and, besides, the guidelines were all there in the contract.

I knew that I enjoyed people, liked being around them, and felt that my work was sharper when exposed to the challenge of conflicting opinions. At the *Chicago Daily News,* I realized I would have the opportunity to compare notes with correspondents working in foreign and domestic fields.

So I elected to work at the office and show my ideas to McArdle. Any suggestions he makes are to improve the cartoon and sharpen the idea, even if he disagrees completely with my stand on a particular issue. He often kids me about my long-winded captions. I would miss very much not working with him.

I hope the last editorial group I will have to consort with is the one at the *Chicago Daily News.* An impressive group from whom I am constantly learning, it's a real liberal, conservative mix, probably somewhat heavier on the liberal side. Daryle Feldmeir and Ken McArdle, whom I've mentioned, are part of the editorial conferences.

Then there is the chief editorial writer, Fred Pannwitt, a tall, slim balding guy who wears glasses and is about my age, fifty-six. Fred's the conservative one on the editorial board. I can understand that—he was an officer on a mine-sweeper during World War II and that's no place for a thrashing-around-in-the-water radical.

Fred taught journalism at Columbia University. He trained at the Chicago City News Bureau, the training ground for all great Chicago newspapermen, and was with the Associated Press. He has been with the *Chicago Daily News* for twenty-seven years as reporter, rewrite man, assistant city editor, editorial writer and chief editorial writer.

Another member of the editorial staff is Gerry Robichaud, a guy of about sixty-one, who's part Indian, French, English, and a lot of other nationalities, although with no Italian blood. That's good, because his temperament couldn't take any more hot pepper: Gerry always wants to knock heads together. I would say he's liberal but Gerry would be the first to thrash a liberal who tried to do something rotten.

Gerry was Washington Bureau Manager and later Chief of the old *Chicago Sun* and when Field bought the *Chicago Times* Gerry became Chief of the *Sun-Times* Washington Bureau. He was a Latin American foreign correspondent from 1959 to 1965, then opened a bureau in Los Angeles in 1965 and started writing editorials for the *Daily News* in 1966.

At the editorial conferences I find Gerry extremely knowledgeable, an expert on every goddamn thing. A specialist in local, state, and national politics, he also has a great interest in and knowledge of law and courts, and of economics and Latin American affairs.

And he's also a very angry middle-aged man, which I find beautiful. Beautiful.

Joe Geshwiler is the youngest member of our editorial family. He came to the editorial department about two years ago from the news staff. He writes editorials and is in charge of the selection of letters that are used daily.

Myron Beckenstein is another younger man. He had the job Joe now holds and currently is a copy editor. Myron, a quiet, witty guy, looked up at Mauldin one time when Bill and I were returning from lunch and said, "Mauldin? Mauldin? Weren't you killed in World War II?"

Myron and I have walked three miles to work every day for years. I keep trying to trip the officious pup, but he's too fast for me.

Everybody has a "Red Baron" in his life. Mine is Nick Shuman, Piper Cub artillery spotter pilot in World War II.

Nick is now National and Foreign Editor, a job that affords him great satisfaction. Nick has a long newspaper background in Chicago, and just before this job, he was doing "idea hunching"—coming up with ideas that would add something different to the paper. When he left that to join the foreign desk he said he felt he was finally coming back to the newspaper business. With some of the things that are going on in our country these days I'm tempted to unleash Nick Shuman and his Piper Cub on those foul balls on the Potomac.

In this business of liberal-conservative or whatever labelling, I sometimes find myself cast in strange roles. One day at the office, Fred Pannwitt, chief editorial writer, had a phone call from an Irate. The Irate was yelling loud and clear about a Crime Commission report carried in the paper the day before about mob-affiliated businesses in which there had been quite a few Italian names. The Irate, a schoolteacher of Italian descent, screamed at Pannwitt that the *Chicago Daily News* was anti-Italian or it wouldn't have run the story. Pannwitt calmly told the screamer that he knew for a fact that the *Daily News* was not anti-Italian, but that the story had simply reported on a news release issued by the Crime Commission. He pointed out that all the papers had reported on it. The Irate wouldn't let up. Finally, in desperation, Pannwitt told the schoolteacher that there was a political cartoonist of Italian descent on our paper, who was right there in the office. He suggested that the Irate talk to the Italian-American cartoonist. There was a moment of silence and then, "I'm not talking to any Uncle Tom."

Laughing, Fred hung up and called me "Uncle Tom." My first reaction was indignation, then on reflection, I translated it into Italian. "Si," uncle; "Tomasso," Tom—I was a "Si Tomasso." I really had to laugh.

The newsmen at the *Daily News* are something else. Mike Royko, for instance, to me is what newspapers are all about.

ROYKO

CASSIUS

Mike is Chicago's ombudsman with clout.

When some ordinary Chicagoan has a legitimate beef about something, he or she knows better than to appeal to the city fathers for relief. The great majority of Chicagoans just suffer in silence, but some appeal to Royko and if the beef is a valid one and Mike takes it on, the shit usually hits the fan. He certainly gets action. In the first place, Mike is such a damned good reporter that he always thoroughly checks out any beef he writes about. In the six years I've been here I haven't seen Mike with egg on his face once, although I *have* seen people go to jail, get sued, or slink away with their tails between their legs, feigning innocence in croaking voices.

Royko is your really average Chicagoan—playing softball in the park, pitching and managing. He's a slugger, both on the ballfield and in bars. He knows the town inside out, knows all the good guys and the bad characters around and is absolutely fearless. Studs Terkel always gets worried when Mike starts to tackle the hoods in town. I have a feeling it's the hoods who do the worrying.

Mike's great success with his best-selling book, *Boss,* about Mayor Daley, hasn't changed a thing as far as his day-to-day life is concerned. His column is everything to him, and thank God, because it's such a great force in our town. Every city should have a Royko.

He loves Italian food and eats everything in sight at Sammy Tuffano's, a restaurant in Chicago's Little Italy. Or what's left of Chicago's Little Italy after Daley and his banana heads got done cementing most of it over.

Mike's a great guitar player and also a connoisseur of fine wine, but don't tell nobody.

Then there's Peter Lisagor, one of my oldest and most trusted friends. From the time he was my editor on *Stars and Stripes* we've never lost contact with each other. Whenever I've had a professional decision to make throughout the years, I've always contacted Pete to get his views on the change I was contemplating.

Some guys just have it and Pete does. He is recognized as one of the best newspapermen writing on politics today.

Before going to the Washington Bureau for the *Chicago Daily News,* Pete was the United Nations Correspondent in New York City and he is now Bureau Chief in Washington.

When I run into him at the countless national political conventions we've attended, he's usually working his butt off. But he loves to tell stories and jokes and will always take time out for that.

He's been on countless TV programs—Face the Nation, Meet the Press, the Martin Agronsky Show

LISAGOR

in Washington, D.C., The Week in Review. His face and voice are instantly recognized and because of this exposure, Pete is very big with little old ladies. Everyplace I go, when someone mentions that I'm with the *Chicago Daily News,* some sweet old lady will ask whether I know Peter Lisagor. When I say that I do, she will cozy up and with an aged Marilyn Monroe throatiness, whisper, "Will you tell him I *adore* him?"

Three of the women I work with make you wonder what the hell all this man-woman stuff is. One can never think of them as "just women" when reading their stories, because they're so good at what they do. All *I* can think about is how good the stories are.

Lois Wille of the *Chicago Daily News* won a Pulitzer in 1963 and has done at least ten things that should have gotten her another Pulitzer since then. Georgie Anne or Gee Gee Geyer is a first-rate foreign correspondent on the *Daily News* and Patricia O'Brien on the Chicago *Sun-Times* who won a Nieman Fellowship this year and also published a first-rate book, *The Woman Alone,* is just as impressive.

It's a pleasure to be associated with reporters of their caliber.

When I arrived in Chicago in the fall of 1967 I found out that my office was about fifteen feet away from Bill Mauldin's. The first time I had met Bill was in Paris in 1945 when he was en route to a meeting with General Patton. I was on the Paris edition of *Stars and Stripes* and Bill was on the Mediterranean edition. I was a fan of his and was delighted to meet him. He looked like such a kid. I'm six years older than he is and he *still* looks like a kid to me. Some kid!

In the ensuing years, since he lived in Rockland County, New York, and I was in Cos Cob, I ran into him every so often. Being with him again here in Chicago was very pleasant. We started to scuff around together most of the time.

MAULDIN

I'll never forget the first few days. Bill gave me a rundown on who was worth a shit around town and who wasn't. He's always been a shrewd judge of character. He mentioned one name and said, "I recognized him as a natural enemy the first time I saw him."

People recognized Bill everywhere we went. One day, in a restaurant, I asked Bill if he had a match. He had stopped smoking years before, but before he could say "no," the guy sitting at the next table, who had overheard me asking for a match, struck one, held it out in my general direction and gabbled, "I'm a great fan of yours, Mr. Mauldin."

The match held out to me was bobbing around like a cork. I had to bring Bill's fan back to earth by telling him he was burning my goddamn nose.

During the first few months I was in town, Bill used to phone for a table at Ric's. One day he was busy and asked if I'd phone, but I said he'd better do it because they wouldn't know me. So Bill picked up the phone and got a new waiter. I heard him ask for a table, pause, and say, "Mauldin." Pause. "M-A-U . ." I broke up, rolled around the floor; my famous friend finished spelling his name.

Last year Bill married a lovely young blonde named Chris, who had been an editorial assistant very popular with *Daily News* people. She's still very loyal to us all. I was Bill's best man when they were married, so I am, in Italian, their *cumpá* or god-father.

One of the areas in which I have always had a very deep interest is the role of the military in our country. The vast amounts of money expended in this area have a direct bearing on the quality of life in this country. I realize of course that we need a strong defense and do not need costly errors and stupidity. But we must still ask whether we will spend for bombs, bullets and blunders, or opt in favor of better air, water, education, hospitals, and care for the elderly.

Bill McGaffin of the *Chicago Daily News* Washington Bureau has been enormously helpful to me in my military education. He's covered the Pentagon and has been a responsible observer of our military for many years.

Many of the cartoons that I've drawn on the military have been inspired by McGaffin. I want him to know how helpful he's been to me in my work.

The Chicago scene has been a powerful and positive breeding ground for ideas for me, although contact with other cartoonists has been much less than it was in New York and Connecticut.

One notable exception to the cartoonist desert in Chicago is Morrie Brickman. When I arrived in Chicago six years ago, the cartoonist I most wanted to meet was the creator of *The Small Society.*

Brickman does some of the sharpest satirical work in comic strips today.

Morrie's a Chicagoan who started professionally by rendering, that is, drawing in halftone, wash or Zip–a–Tone, of shoes in advertisements. It was as dull as the Disney assembly line.

The Small Society is now deservedly successful. One of my favorites from it was drawn during the terrible battles between the youngsters and the police in Chicago during the 1968 Democratic Convention. It shows a group of kids carrying signs saying "Peace," "Love." Two policemen, watching them, are saying, "Oh, oh, here comes trouble!"

Morrie is married to Shirley, a great woman and terrific cook, whose chicken soup has kept Morrie brave, clean and reverent.

One of the best places to meet interesting people in Chicago, whether they're cartoonists, writers, theatre people, movie stars, in advertising or just plain folks is a place called Riccardo's, a well-known Italian restaurant with a long tradition as a meeting place in Chicago. After getting my idea for the day, I always used to go to lunch there. Four of us had a permanent table at Booth Number One: Bill Mauldin, Jack Star, and Dave Murray.

Jack Star was born, raised, got married and has worked in Chicago all his life—fifty years, give or take one.

He was a reporter on the *Chicago Times* and the *Chicago Sun-Times.* He joined *Look* magazine over twenty years ago and was their Midwest Bureau Chief when they folded.

Riding around Chicago with Jack gives you an idea of the enormous problems facing large cities. He showed me the movements of the different ethnic groups, the jails, the hospitals. He pointed out the areas where the aged poor stay holed in their houses, afraid to venture out into the streets—with damned good reason, for they get clobbered in broad daylight for the pittance of the welfare dollar they carry on them.

Dave Murray and I were on the *New York Herald Tribune* together and when it folded he came to the *Chicago Sun-Times.* The cast that used to be on Dave's broken leg is probably the only cast in existence with cartoons of Agnew, Nixon, and Johnson drawn by three Pulitzer Prize winners.

A political reporter at heart, in Chicago he gave editorial writing a good try but it wasn't for him. His heart is with politics and so we lost him at the table at Ric's—he's now happy as hell in the Washington Bureau of the *Sun-Times.*

The lunches were always very lively and informative affairs but the group broke up about a year ago when *Look* folded and Jack Star began to freelance out of his home. About the same time, Dave

Murray went to Washington and Bill Mauldin started spending more time in Santa Fe with his new wife.

There was a constant flow of characters who used to drop by our table. Herbert Lawrence Block or Herblock, the great cartoonist on the *Washington Post,* comes to Chicago from time to time to visit family and friends and also to do a little missionary work for whatever is his latest book. He was originally a Chicagoan and his first job was on my paper, the *Chicago Daily News.* He was also my predecessor at NEA where he worked for ten years.

Herb is the owner of two Pulitzer Prizes and a mention, which he received in 1973, when the *Washington Post* got the Pulitzer. Cited along with him were Bernstein and Woodward, the two young reporters who broke the Watergate affair wide open, and a *Washington Post* editorial writer, Roger Wilkens.

But Herb has so many other awards and honorary degrees that I'll let it go at that, because he's a modest man and, besides, I refuse to give the opposition any more than that.

We've been friends for a long time, but after knowing him for over twenty years, he *still* can surprise a guy. He casually mentioned something last year about "us Italians." I was puzzled and told him so.

Herb then told me that although his father was

Jewish, his mother was of Italian descent. His maternal grandparents came from Genoa, Italy. *"Mannaggia*! Thatsa nice!" I thought.

Herb's office, not his nice new one, but his old office, used to be loaded with newspapers, magazines, awards, old shoes, toy guns that sent out a little POP! or BANG! banner, toy swords and Snoopy dogs. One day when Herb was in Chicago at Riccardo's with a group of us, my wife, who was seated beside him, noticed his inside jacket pocket when he bent over to reach for something. Karen said, "My God, your pocket looks like your office."

HERBLOCK

Herb looked at the wallets, papers, credit cards, pens and pencils affectionately and answered, "Yeah, and I was thinking of having the pocket panelled in knotty pine."

One Riccardo's regular was Studs Terkel who's usually all over town puffing on his cigar, waxing indignant about Vietnam, Daley, Nixon, Cambodia.

Studs is sixty-one. He came to Chicago from New York when he was eleven.

During the McCarthy period Terkel had a TV show and did a lot of radio acting. But because Studs' voice came over the air like a gangster's, he never got the long parts that the good guy had on radio. Since he was always a bad-ass, he had to get his comeuppance, so Studs always wound up knocked off and there went the job. Studs claims he never had tenure in radio.

Studs was always outspoken on civil rights and liberties, and like so many others, he suddenly found employment hard to come by. So everyone in town was happy to see him come back with his books *Giants of Jazz, Division Street: USA,* and his best seller *Hard Times.* He now does taped interviews on FM radio on his program, "Stud's Place".

He's still very outspoken and would put it all on the line again, if he had to.

Bob Cromie, *Chicago Tribune* columnist, and

Herman Kogan, the Editor of *Showcase,* the arts section of the *Chicago Sun-Times,* started out together as reporters on the *Chicago Tribune.* Through the years they've been close friends, chairing and introducing literary events around town, sharing the honors or the awards they're always getting. Once they even did a book together, an excellent one on the Chicago fire.

One or the other or both usually stopped by Riccardo's to talk on any given afternoon, frequently with an author or celebrity in tow.

Bob Cromie is a sturdily built man about five feet ten, with sandy hair turning grey. He does three TV shows and a newspaper column and he has the kindest eyes in Chicago. They mirror the concern he feels for every unfortunate creature, human or animal. He calls me up, outraged, when he hears about hunters beating white baby seals to death with clubs. He calls on behalf of Chicago kids who are not getting enough to eat, or if a Christmas is going by in which some kids won't have toys.

His concern spills over to his TV programs. He never conducts cardboard interviews—he's too concerned about the one who's being interviewed and his or her subject. And he doesn't short-change: he bones up, he reads, he does his home-work.

He was a war correspondent for the *Chicago Tribune* during World War II and then was their

Book Editor for many years. Now he's almost become a *paisane,* a countryman—he just bought a house in Italy.

Herman Kogan is compact, brown-eyed and balding. His newspaper career goes back to his days on the *Chicago Tribune.*

Herman started *Panorama,* the very successful arts section of the *Daily News.* After that, he was Assistant General Manager of the news and news-papers division of WFLD TV station where he helped produce three Emmy award winning shows. He then became the Book Editor of the *Chicago Sun-Times* and is now the Editor of the new *Sun-*

Times arts section.

Herman drops by my office from time to time and gives me lessons on Chicago, the fire, the newspaper tales, the politicians, and the incredible characters, past and present, of this incredible city. If it wasn't Herman telling the stories, I wouldn't believe them, and he doesn't just tell you about all of it—he acts out all the parts.

All three men nearly always have someone in tow, doing the Grand Tour of the talk shows from coast to coast. Such quick restaurant encounters are a great way to be educated, if you want to hear how tough it is to be an author and what dolts publishers are. To know what the books were about, you had to see or hear the writers on the shows. In Chicago, you can flip the switch and find authors on Book Beat, Kup's Show, the Today Show, Studs Terkel's Radio Interview, and Kennedy and Company. Yet you do think back to those lunch conversation complaints when you hear on the newscasts that big name authors are peddling their books from pushcarts in New York to make the point that, after hustling all over the country talking themselves blue, the public still can't find their books in the stores to buy.

But for me the serious business is coming up with those cartoons. Five days a week, week in, week out, year in, year out, this cartoonist goes to the well, hoping to come up with a usable idea.

To anyone with any sense, coming up with a good idea is a frightening, mysterious and thoroughly unpredictable process. To a cartoonist, it is all that and more. A cartoonist's ass is on the line.

How does one go about isolating an idea, tracking it down and with a victorious "Yip!" capturing it, to have and to hold forever? After all, if it's a great idea, it will be referred to, will be reprinted in books and magazines, and become a part of the historical chronicling of your country.

You'd think that an idea, knowing such wonderful things were going to happen to it, would fight to be captured. But no, the idea knows that whatever glory is achieved will be shared with the cartoonist. The idea and the artist will be linked irrevocably, and great ideas are very fussy about the company they keep.

My good friend Jacob Burck, a Pulitzer Prize cartoonist on the *Chicago Sun-Times,* and a scarred veteran of the hunt, refers to the entrapment of an idea as the Creative Grind.

The creative grind starts off every morning by trying to keep awake. The cartoonists' boneyard is littered with the casualties of this first hurdle.

You try to keep some lively banter going, early on in the morning, in the hope that someone will come up with a line you can use. This almost never works, but what the hell.

At this stage, your main concern is to keep from looking frightened. So you bury your head in a newspaper to give passersby the impression that your look of concern, bordering on fright, has to do with something you are reading about.

The real problem each day is not the almost impossible quest for a great idea; the more pressing problem is to determine the topic.

My method is to make a list of possible topics down the right-hand side of my layout pad of subjects or stories in the news. Some days there'll be three or four, some days eight, nine, ten. In the news business there are days when nothing seems to be going on, and other days when you're smothered with important things happening all at once.

After I run my list of possible topics down the side, I start doodling. Not the aimless, decorative, geometric doodling that Presidents, Cabinet officers, and tycoons indulge in, but big time, important doodling with *real* cartoon figures and scenes.

The object is to constantly occupy yourself with writing lines, drawing figures, just anything, to get in the creative or idea-hunting mood. This works for me. I can just *feel* when the lines and doodled figures are getting warm, indicating that a usable idea is in the immediate vicinity.

Other times you *know* you've got a cold hand and it's going to be a long, long day.

Feeling deeply about an injustice or a social outrage doesn't make you a political cartoonist. You have to be incensed enough and professional enough to come up with a good idea and a good drawing within your deadline time limit.

Of course, no one I know comes up with a great cartoon every day. I consider two, or possibly three, very good ones out of the five done a week a more than respectable average.

If a cartoonist has trouble doing one good one out of five a week, he is relegated to what Bill Mauldin calls the pants pressers in the business.

The fastest time in which I conceived and finished a cartoon was just under one hour. When Dag Hammarskjold, Secretary General of the United Nations, was killed in an airplane crash in Africa, I was with the Newspaper Enterprise Association. My editor, Boyd Lewis, told me when I arrived that morning that we were going to airmail stories, backgrounds, editorials and my cartoon to NEA clients immediately. I had an hour to come up with an idea and a finished cartoon.

What I had going for me was an enormous regard for Hammarskjold. An indefatigable worker for peace, he didn't just talk about it. He lived, breathed, and worked for it. He was an activist. I was shocked and deeply grieved by his tragic death. In a world filled with armaments and trigger-happy world leaders, this man had stood out like a beacon and now the beacon was extinguished.

I simply drew a corner of the United Nations building; it could have been the corner of a headstone. Behind the stark white of the building, I sketched a jet-black sky. In the lower right, at the base of the building, was a female peace figure, face in hands, head bent. The caption of my cartoon was simply, "MY SON, MY SON."

My deep feelings about Hammarskjold's death must have come through in the cartoon, for I have never received such a reaction, before or since. The phone never stopped ringing, and people even cried when they spoke to me. Letters and telegrams came for days afterward. Editors from all over the country wrote to my editors, saying that phone calls to their papers had started the moment their papers were on the street.

Ralph Bunche wrote that the cartoon had touched him and everyone he had spoken to at the U.N. He requested the original of the cartoon and told me that the U.N. wanted to place the cartoon permanently outside Dag Hammarskjold's office on the 37th floor of the Secretariat building. Boyd and

'My Son, My Son'

I presented the original to Dr. Bunche and, as far as I know, the cartoon is there today.

Before 1961 I used to doodle ideas on the backs of envelopes, scraps of paper and yellow copy paper. After working up an idea, I'd crumple the paper and throw it away. I found that most of my colleagues worked the same way. Many times I had the germ of an idea which with more work would be usable, but the ideas were thrown out with the scraps of papers. Since even half-formed ideas are invaluable, I decided to use layout pads for the gestating periods. By dating each page, it turned out to be a sort of log of historical and personal events.

After reading newspapers for about three hours every morning, I jot down the most important topics of the day in a column on the right-hand side of the page. (Just for the record, a layout pad has sixty semi-transparent pages and the pad I use is nine by eleven.)

I will go through two, three and sometimes four sheets of doodling thumbnail sketches of people and scenes. On some delightful and rare days, I hit on a usable idea immediately. When you have your day's idea smack, right away, you can then afford to work on perfecting ideas for the next hour or two, trying to get a better one, without breathing hard.

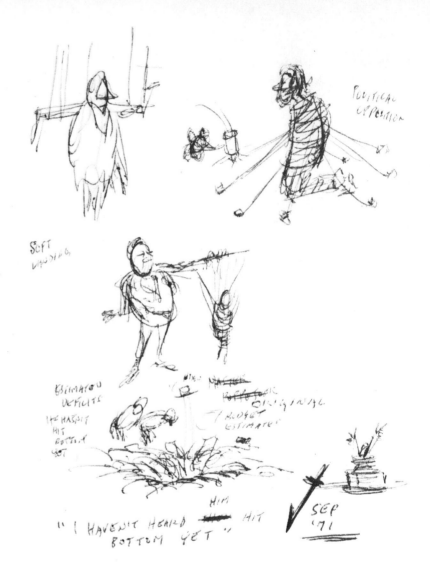

99

Some days you really sweat it. It seems all your creative gears are frozen. Your indignation on so many subjects results in nothing more than a pitiful unimaginative bleat. That's when Bill Mauldin, who works down the hall, is likely to come in, dying to tell me about his idea for a cartoon. But he won't tell what his idea is if I don't have mine for the day. He'll just walk off smugly, saying, "I've got a lulu!" Then of course all I can think is, "He's got a lulu . . . he's got a lulu." On days like this my batting average declines perceptibly.

One of the dividends that accrues from working with a layout pad is that quite often one of the figures or scenes I'm drawing is absolutely meaningless until my eye catches another little scene on the page. Damn, sometimes the two elements make up an idea!

A terribly embarrassing thing happened to me one time when I hit on an idea this way. I was working on some ideas for *Punch* magazine. One of the little sketches I did was of Adam and Eve in which Adam had the apple in his hand. I couldn't come up with an amusing line so I moved to another part of the page and drew other scenes, forgetting Adam and Eve. One of the scenes I drew was of an astronaut coming down the ladder of a spaceship that had landed on another planet. I couldn't think of anything funny. My eye caught the

Adam and Eve sketch. I redrew this guy coming out of the spaceship. This time, I had him running toward Adam and Eve, as Adam was about to bite the apple. He was waving his arms and my caption was, "Good Heavens! No! No! No!"

Punch bought the cartoon and it was published. Some weeks later I received a letter from the cartoon editor of *Punch*. It seemed that he had received a strong letter from a New York lawyer flatly accusing me of stealing the idea from Whitney Darrow, Jr.

Punch obviously agreed with the lawyer and wrote me a scorching letter indicating that they frowned on that sort of thing. I could feel the blood rushing to my face as I read the letter. I was alone in my home when I received it and I was red-faced and furious that anyone would accuse me of stealing ideas.

So I wrote a scorching letter in return to *Punch* asking how they dared to accuse me, etc., etc. I told them that Whitney Darrow, Jr., was a friend of mine, and that I wouldn't stoop to anything like that even with an enemy. Furthermore, I told them to keep their check for the cartoon and that I would stop contributing to their magazine.

A little later *Punch*'s cartoon editor replied, "Received your incandescent letter . . ." and apologized for his intemperate letter. Since they did

"*For heaven's sake! No! No! No!*"

PUNCH, December 31 1958

apologize and agreed that my integrity was not to be questioned in the future, I agreed to continue contributing.

The following week I ran into Whitney at a Dutch Treat Club luncheon. I told him what had happened and how humiliated I had felt about the whole thing. Darrow told me that every time he sat down at the drawing board he wondered if he or someone else hadn't already drawn the cartoon he was working on.

"By the way, John, what was the cartoon they squawked about?" he asked.

I described the cartoon. There was a long pause.

"Jesus, they used that on the cover of my book," he said.

To this day I haven't seen that damned book.

Things like that happen from time to time to cartoonists thousands of miles apart. Just recently I did a cartoon based on Burt Reynolds' nude centerfold in *Cosmopolitan* magazine. It showed a taxpayer, nude, in the centerfold of a city, state and federal tax information booklet. It had no caption. Then I saw a reprint of a Paul Conrad cartoon which had a naked taxpayer in the center of etc., etc., and it had no caption. I called Paul in Los Angeles from Chicago, and asked when he had done the cartoon. He couldn't remember, so I spoke to the people at the Chicago Bureau of the

Los Angeles Times and they sent me the editorial page containing the cartoon. Both cartoons had appeared the morning of Friday, March 31, 1972— Conrad and I had drawn identical cartoons on the same day in Los Angeles and Chicago.

Whether what I come up with is unique to me or not, since good ideas are what a cartoon is all about, I once tried to track down why one day there would be a surplus of genius and another day a deficit.

I jotted down the hours of sleep I had had, what I had had for breakfast, whether I had walked to work, taken a bus or driven my car. I even kept track of whether there had been sex the night before. Hell, I wanted to be scientific about it all, so I left no stone unturned. After writing down everything I could possibly remember about what I had done to lead myself into a great idea day, I found the conditions varied enormously.

On one great idea day, I had a blistering hangover; on another I hadn't had a drink in a week. Once I was on a diet. No matter how rigidly I adhered to the schedule that would theoretically produce a great idea day, it just never worked. So I guess it has to do with something even more scientific, like the phase of the moon or the exact amount of lichee nuts in the city, or just how many lushes went on the wagon in the 43rd Ward.

103

Anyway, now that I've given up my quest for The Great Short Cut to Easy Ideas, you'll find me any morning at my board on the *Chicago Daily News*, smoking, drinking coffee, shaking, biting my pen and acting just like any other successful cartoonist.

After lunch, I return to the paper and go ahead with the finished drawing.

The length of time spent on the drawing should depend only on how intricate or involved the idea is. But there are days when you just feel like drawing up a storm and that can be dangerous, since you can get carried away with technique and manage to smother your idea. The great Rollin Kirby, political cartoonist for the old *New York World,* observed many years ago that " . . . a good idea has carried many an indifferent drawing to glory but never has a good drawing rescued a bad idea from oblivion." The only possible excuse for a drawing better than the idea is when the idea is so bad that smothering it with a *tour de force* drawing is just showing the reader a little mercy. Then at least your lousy idea gets a loving burial.

While it did take just one hour to do the Dag Hammarskjold cartoon, unless you get lucky, it takes a couple of hours.

The longest time I've labored to come up with an idea was eight hours. It's only happened once, but it felt like being in quicksand. Slowly, ever so slowly, sinking, sinking. The more I struggled, the deeper I became mired. I can't even remember what idea I finally came up with, but laboring that long, I'm sure I just brought forth a mouse.

One deeply guarded cartoonists' secret is the pot-boiler or evergreen, which is a cartoon that can be used any time. I always keep one or two of this type of cartoon tucked away on a back shelf. When I want to get away for a week or so, I'll start building up a backlog of evergreens. They're usually socio-political gag cartoons, like the kind I used to do for *Punch* magazine.

Occasionally, though, an evergreen hits on target. One I did a few years ago showed a painter painting a sunset while sitting on someone's private beach. A sign in the right-hand corner announced this to one and all. The skinny-legged tycoon-type owner of the private beach was screaming at the artist.

A few weeks later a man phoned me at the *Chicago Daily News.* He asked if I was one of the three men who had been painting on his private beach. I didn't know what the hell he was talking about until he described my cartoon. But as it turned out, he had chased the painters off his beach about a month before I had drawn my cartoon. He seemed a little disappointed.

Before he hung up, he told me he was a fan of

"CAN'T YOU READ? THAT'S MY SUNSET YOU'RE PAINTING"

mine. He terminated our conversation with, "You're absolutely welcome to paint on my private beach any time you want to, Mr. Fischetti." Unexpected fringe benefits do turn up.

In a way it wasn't so unusual, though, because Chicago is an incredibly friendly town for a cartoonist to work in. People think nothing of calling you up, chatting away like backyard neighbors, telling you they agree or disagree with your position on some political issue. Quite often they contribute ideas which I generally turn down as gracefully as I can.

About the only cartoon idea submitted to me that I've used was a twist on the movie, "The Russians are Coming! The Russians are Coming!" occasioned by President Nixon's visit to the Soviet Union. A Mr. LeMieux sent in the idea.

But not all fans are so enthusiastic. Right in the middle of writing this book I had a mild coronary. While I was in the hospital, my paper and my syndicate, Publishers-Hall, reprinted some old cartoons with the line under them, "John Fischetti is ill and we are reprinting some of his 1972 cartoons."

In my mail was a letter from a fan who had ripped my cartoon out of a Carolina newspaper. After reading the line under the cartoon (page 107, bottom left) about my being ill, he added a comment of his own and sent it on to me.

With fans like that out there, I could hardly wait to get well and turn them all on again. And it's not an unusual occurrence. These are other love notes from fans.

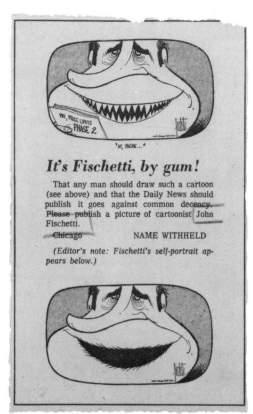

It's Fischetti, by gum!

That any man should draw such a cartoon (see above) and that the Daily News should publish it goes against common decency. Please publish a picture of cartoonist John Fischetti.

Chicago   NAME WITHHELD

(Editor's note: Fischetti's self-portrait appears below.)

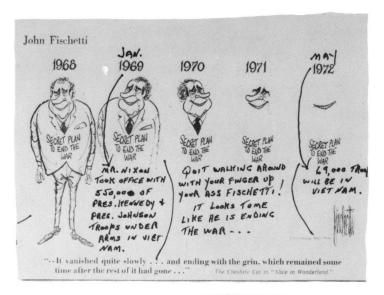

John Fischetti

1968   JAN. 1969   1970   1971   MAY 1972

SECRET PLAN TO END THE WAR (×5)

MR. NIXON TOOK OFFICE WITH 550,000 OF PRES. KENNEDY & PRES. JOHNSON TROOPS UNDER ARMS IN VIET NAM.

QUIT WALKING AROUND WITH YOUR FINGER UP YOUR ASS FISCHETTI! IT LOOKS TO ME LIKE HE IS ENDING THE WAR...

69,000 TROOPS WILL BE IN VIETNAM.

"...It vanished quite slowly . . . and ending with the grin, which remained some time after the rest of it had gone . . ." *The Cheshire Cat in "Alice in Wonderland."*

THIS GOVERNMENT HATER IS DOING HIS BEST TO TRY TO DESTROY OUR GOOD U.S. GOVERNMENT.

John Fischetti   (THE (BASTARD) COMMUNIST

SEND HIM TO HANOI.

NEW YORK VICTORY   WINS OVER TYDINGS, GORE   STATEHOUSES   LOST   ILLINOIS DEFEAT   TEXAS DEFEAT   FLORIDA   CALIFORNIA   SENATE LOSSES

Samson & Co.

EARLY TO BED EARLY TO RISE...   A STITCH IN TIME...   FOR WANT OF A NAIL...   BUDGET DEFICIT   WASTE NOT WANT NOT   GOP

"Funny, you don't look Republican"

Editor's Note. John Fischetti is ill. Until he is able to resume work, this newspaper is using previously published cartoons.

Now isn't that just too sad. What is your alleged affliction? Hydrophobia, I presume. You deserve whatever you have, you lousy stinking swine.

WALLACE DEMAGOGUERY

"Thish shtuff pashes wi' clying folors"

With the continued help of good and loyal followers such as yourself, Comrade Fischetti, our cherished goal of ONE WORLD COMMUNISM will soon be achieved. Keep up the good work. The entire Party salutes you. Chou.

107

Every
fish-head
needs a
crown—
from your
friend—

MAULDIN · 1969

THE PULITZER

When I sit down in the morning to begin work on a political cartoon I am part of all the people I've worked with, part close Italian family, and part talent. I bring this to my drawing board and I feel very confident and dream impossible dreams for mankind. Sometimes it seems others believe those dreams, too.

Just about every other day some youngster from high school or college sends a letter or a long form for me to fill out, asking about my work and where and when I started, and always, how effective I think my cartoons are.

It's really impossible to gauge the effect my cartoons are having on people. Every once in a while, someone will tell me he remembers a cartoon I did five, ten, or fifteen years ago and the amazing thing is that he'll remember the picture, the caption, and the whole sense of the cartoon—everything.

I can only assume from incidents like this that sometimes I *do* hit someone with an idea that simply never leaves.

I like to believe that perhaps that cartoon he remembers affected a vote of his or in some way, a part of his life.

I'm a professional at doing political cartoons. I was lousy as a soldier, as a student, and probably a few other things. But I'm a damned good political cartoonist and I feel that my cartoons can be part of an effective force to make things a little better for a lot of ordinary people who are worried, perplexed, and concerned about the direction we, as human beings, are going.

I want to be a plus for my fellows before I die rather than a minus. No big deal, just that. And occasionally it seems I'm getting close to the target.

Monday, May 5th, 1969, started the way most Mondays do, with my trying to shift into a higher gear at the office after an indolent weekend.

I already had an idea when I arrived, so instead of working on ideas that morning, I went right to work on drawing the cartoon. About one, I broke for lunch with Bill Mauldin and David Murray. Then, returning from lunch, I put the finishing touches on my cartoon and hustled it down to the engraving room. I picked up a cup of coffee from the vending machine and returned to my office to settle down to a quiet afternoon.

At about two-thirty, there was a commotion out in the hall: voices and the pounding of lots of feet coming closer and closer. My name was threaded in with the other sounds.

I thought it was a goddamn lynching party, so I reached out for my metal T square, prepared to take a couple with me if I was going down.

At my doorway Daryle Feldmeir, then Managing Editor, Roy Fisher, Editor, and Ken McArdle, my Editorial Page Editor, appeared, beaming, with a horde of people behind them.

They blurted out, "Fischetti . . . You won the Pulitzer . . . . "

I started to rise from my chair, got half-way up with my knees shaking, then plopped back into the chair and said, "No shit!"

I was pounded on the back with congratulations and wrestled out to our city room, a long city block away from the ivory tower of my office.

Completely dazed, I saw everyone was there, reporters, editors, copy boys, rewrite men, all standing up and applauding. I didn't know what to do, so I simply bowed from the waist.

A reporter started interviewing me in the middle of this bedlam and pictures were taken.

Reality started to catch up with me and I wanted my wife Karen to know. I excused myself and got back to my office and phoned home. No answer. Someone had phoned Karen from the paper and she was already on the way down.

I went with Hoke Norris, then a *Chicago Daily News* editorial writer, to Riccardo's to hoist one and relax for a moment. The place was empty since the last of the luncheon mob had departed. There the whole atmosphere was totally different from the city room. When Hoke told Bill, the bartender, that I had just won the Pulitzer, Bill only said, "Great! You want lemon with that martini?"

Hoke and I returned to my office where the phone calls were coming in from Washington, California, New York, Connecticut, everywhere. *Newsweek* and *Time* called. Telegrams started coming in and the first one was from my old boss on the *New York Herald Tribune,* Jock Whitney. It was quickly followed by another from Boyd Lewis, who had been my editor at NEA.

JOHN FISCHETTI
CHICAGO DAILY NEWS 401 WABASH CHGO
I KNOW HOW DELIGHTED YOUR MANY H-T FRIENDS MUST BE OVER YOUR
PUTLITZER BUT NONE MORE THAN MRS WHITNEY AND MYSELF. CONGRATULATIONS
JOCK WHITNEY
(24).

WU 1270 (R6-66)

CHICAGO DAILY NEWS

JOHN FISCHETTI

THE PULITZER BOARD HAS DONE ITSELF HONOR BY PICKING A REAL
CARTOONIST AND A GREAT MAN.   WE SHARE IN THE SATISFACTION
YOU AND KAREN MUST FEEL JOHN.   AMORE.

                                                    BOYD

When I came to Chicago, I discovered to my great annoyance that the only thing the name "Fischetti" meant to old-time Chicagoans was a gangster cousin of Capone's. I had vowed that "Fischetti" would come to mean only "political cartoons" in Chicago, and that the other association would be buried. Bill McCormick, a sports writer from my NEA days who has since retired, knew how the story of "the other Fischetti" had bugged me, and in his note of congratulations on my award, he kidded me about the achievements of the Fischettis in Chicago.

Bestelman Associates, Inc. 654 MADISON AVENUE NEW YORK, N.Y. 10021 TEMPLETON 8-7800

May 6, 1969

Mr. John Fischetti
Chicago Daily News
401 N. Wabash
Chicago, Illinois

Dear John,

Congratulations.

Apparently the guy (I believe it was either Bill Shakespeare, **George** Herbert or Boyd Lewis) who said "God's mill grinds slow, but sure" was right. The recognition is long overdue.

Looks like the Fischettis all rise to their greatest heights in Chicago.

Best, as always,

Bill McCormick

The Sons of Italy were also aware of the sorry image the mob days in Chicago had given us Italian-Americans, and I was delighted to see their pride in my accomplishing something on the positive side of the ledger.

phone
CEntral 6-6377

GRAND LODGE OF THE STATE OF ILLINOIS

201 NORTH WELLS STREET
Chicago, Ill. 60606
ROOM 604

May 13, 1969

Mr. Roy M. Fisher
Editor
Chicago Daily News
401 North Wabash Avenue
Chicago, Illinois 60605

Dear Mr. Fisher:

Congratulations to The Chicago Daily News for the 13th Pulitzer Prize Award. We, the members of the Grand Lodge of the State of Illinois, Order Sons of Italy in America, join with all the other members of the Order throughout the United States, in taking great pride in this 13th Award, presented to Mr. John Fischetti, cartoonist extraordinary. His perception in depth, leaves very little doubt of the message intended. His thorough knowledge of the subject matter, before he puts his pen to the drawing board, is sheer genius.

The recognition of John Fischetti, by the Pulitzer Prize Committee, has firmly and indelibly placed him among the many great Italo-Americans who have contributed so much in their outstanding field of endeavors to the people of the United States and throughout the World.

Again our sincerest congratulations to a great staff and to an outstanding newspaper.

Very truly yours,

Martin R. Buccieri
Grand Venerable

MRB:ts

THE LARGEST AMERICAN ORGANIZATION OF PEOPLE OF ITALIAN DESCENT IN THE UNITED STATES OF AMERICA AND CANADA

Some of my friends took a definitely less than respectful attitude toward the whole thing, however.

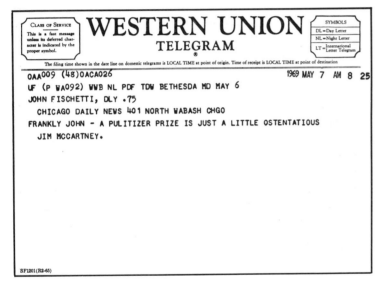

Jim McCartney: Former city editor of the *Chicago Daily News,* now a Washington-based correspondent with the Knight newspapers.

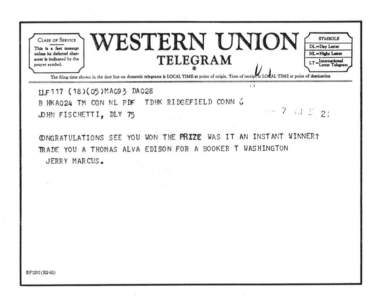

Jerry Marcus: Cartoonist who does the strip, *Trudy.*

Winning the Pulitzer qualified me as brass, at least temporarily. So I was taken to a little nook in the executive section of the Field Newspapers called the Hospitality Suite. Visiting big shots repair to this room with the Field executives to talk of things of moment and to bang back a few. Suddenly there I was banging 'em back with the best of them.

Bailey K. Howard called from California to offer congratulations and then, in talking to Dick Trezevant, the General Manager, he suggested that Dick "spread a little green around for Fischetti." That added up to a substantial raise for the next five years.

Karen and I headed home to find our two sons, Peter and Michael, totally bewildered because some clown had ordered pizzas sent collect to my apartment all day long; my home address had been included in one of the news stories. Over thirty pizzas had arrived and been turned back. The boys didn't know what to make of it.

My wife excitedly asked Michael, "Do you know what happened to your father? He won the Pulitzer Prize!"

Michael, always cool, replied, "Finally."

My older sister Anna was a little more enthusiastic.

Dear "Best in the Country":

That's what the daughter of the woman I work for called you, and of course I heartily agree with her.

It also goes without saying we are so very proud of you.

I have the paper with your picture in it.

I know all the disappointments and how very hard you have worked to reach this goal, and I want to say it couldn't have happened to a nicer brother.

So, I hope and pray that all this will lead to all the things your heart desires.

We love you and are very proud.

Your sis

Anna

Jack Tippit, President of our National Cartoonists
Society, took another approach. The envelope he
sent was addressed:

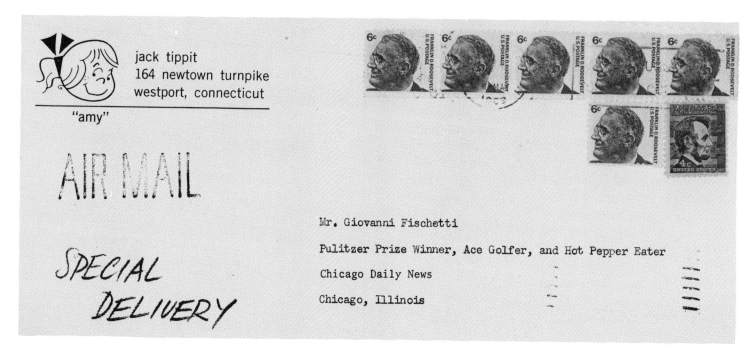

jack tippit
164 newtown turnpike
westport, connecticut

"amy"

AIR MAIL

SPECIAL
DELIVERY

Mr. Giovanni Fischetti

Pulitzer Prize Winner, Ace Golfer, and Hot Pepper Eater

Chicago Daily News

Chicago, Illinois

In congratulating me, another political cartoonist, Charles Bissell of *The Nashville Tennessean,* acknowledged that the permanent change to a horizontal format which I'd made in 1961 when I went to the *Herald Tribune* had popularized the style which most political cartoonists use today. I had made the change after reading several articles about the abysmal state of political cartooning in the United States. It had made me determined to do something to change Americans' attitude toward cartoonists. Although many excellent political cartoonists are known for the horizontal format now, I had always taken some pride in somehow having started a trend back then. The style wasn't original with me—it had been popular in England for some time and used occasionally here—but it meant something special to have another pro comment on it.

IN THE HEART OF TVA

MORNING - SUNDAY — ESTABLISHED 1812

THE NASHVILLE TENNESSEAN

NASHVILLE 1, TENNESSEE

AMON CARTER EVANS
Publisher

May 6, 1969

Dear John:

    Congratulations on winning the Pulitzer! They sure took their time about it though. You should have had it way back when you changed the style that changed the style all around. Anyway it sort of renews my faith in justice.

Sincerely,

Chas.

Chas. O. Bissell

Mike Royko, columnist, author of *Boss* and energetic axer of loutish Chicago heads, sent a unique note of congratulations.

CHICAGO DAILY NEWS

AN INDEPENDENT NEWSPAPER FOUNDED JANUARY 1, 1876

Dear John:

I don't know what this town is coming to when a wop gets on page one without holding his hat over his face, but congratulations.

You and Muldoon are the two greatest artists Chicago has ever had under one roof.

At least since the Everleigh sisters.

Enviously,

MIKE ROYKO

Then when Mike won his Pulitzer in 1972, he spotted me across the crowded newsroom, as everybody was toasting him. He practically ran across the room to hit me with a line he had apparently been honing for three years. He looked me in the eye and said,

"Fischetti, you're a has-been."

President Lyndon B. Johnson also sent a congratulatory note after I received the Pulitzer, and in his letter he invited my wife and me for an evening at the LBJ Ranch. Since Austin, Texas, is not right around the block from Chicago, Illinois, I wrote to President Johnson and asked him what an "evening" would consist of. When would it start and when would it end? The reply was that he'd like us to arrive, have lunch and dinner, stay the night and leave the following morning.

My paper picked up the tab for the flight and Karen and I flew to Austin. One of the President's staff, Mrs. Willie Day Taylor, was there with an automobile for the sixty-seven mile trip to the ranch. Half-way there, Willie Day seemed to be trying to say something, not too successfully. I sensed something was amiss. I asked her if there had been a change in plans. She replied affirmatively and said that now we were just to have lunch and return home after that. I was furious. I motioned to my wife with my thumb, signaling "Let's go the hell back." She shook her head and motioned us forward. I'm glad she did because it turned out to be quite an experience.

President Johnson was a most gracious host. He greeted us at the door dressed in slacks and a polo shirt. He had put on quite a bit of weight. There were just six of us at the dining room table. Karen

AUSTIN, TEXAS

Dear Mr. Fischetti:

My congratulations to the judges of the Pulitzer Awards for selecting you as a recipient. I concur wholeheartedly in their choice.

This honor which you have earned will add even more interest to the cartoon display we are planning, since you have been most generous with your originals. I do hope that you are planning to visit the Library in 1971.

My very best wishes for your continued success.

Sincerely,

Mr. John R. Fischetti
Editorial Cartoonist
Chicago Daily News
401 North Wabash
Chicago, Illinois 60611

May 22, 1969

to the right of the President, a boyhood chum of Johnson's to the right of Karen, and to his right, a Mrs. Boozer, a young attractive secretary, whose husband was a serviceman in Vietnam. To the President's left, Willie Day Taylor, and to her left, me.

We ate simply: huge hamburgers, salad, and peaches and cream. President Johnson poured a veritable Niagara of thick, rich cream over his peaches and urged us to help ourselves to the cream. It was fresh from the farm, he said, as was everything at the table.

I started questioning him about his retirement, about how he felt now, being so far from the center of power that he had occupied so prominently for so many years. He replied that between establishing his library, writing his book and being right in the middle of a TV interview program, he hardly noticed that things had slowed down much.

I brought up Vietnam and pointed out how badly things were going in our own country. I mentioned that our cities were going up in flames, that terrible dissension was eating at all Americans, that there were badly neglected needs, in hospitals, schools, transportation, and among the poor of our cities.

After about seven or eight questions and seven or eight heated replies, President Johnson, red-faced, tapped the table with his large index finger and said,

"That'll be the last question on *that* topic, Mr. Fischetti."

His last answer to my last question was that there wasn't anything the people of this country couldn't do, providing they had the will to do it. They could support the war in Vietnam totally, they could make their cities and towns places of beauty and harmony, they could provide for better schools, hospitals, and take care of the poor. He was absolutely convinced they could do it all, provided they had the will.

Things simmered down after we got off those topics, and the President drove Karen and me around the ranch in his large, white convertible, pointing out places of interest to him. I looked at the airstrip on the grounds. It looked haunted. I wished I could have seen it when President Johnson was in office. It must've really hummed.

Karen and I returned to Chicago with memories we'll not forget.

May 13, 1969

Dear Mr. Fischetti:

While looking through some cartoons recently I
noticed one you had drawn for the Chicago Daily
News captioned "All I can say for now is, 'So far,
so good'."

I always enjoy seeing your work and I found this
cartoon particularly witty. If the original drawing
is available, I hope you will let me have the
opportunity to add it to my personal collection.

With my best wishes,

Sincerely,

Richard Nixon

Mr. John Fischetti
Chicago Daily News
401 North Wabash
Chicago, Illinois 60611

P.S. Congratulations on winning a Pulitzer Prize
for your work! I was delighted to see your name on
the list.

President Nixon's approach was in considerable contrast to LBJ's. Thanks to him, I must be the only guy to have received a Pulitzer who was congratulated in a postscript by a President of the United States.

WHY DON'T THEY LIFT THEMSELVES UP BY THEIR OWN BOOTSTRAPS LIKE WE DID?

HORIZONS

"SPEAKING FROM A POSITION OF STRENGTH..."

"IT SHOULDN'T BE HARD FOR EITHER SIDE TO RAISE OUR STANDARD OF LIVING NOW"

" YOU'D *BETTER* BE TOUGH. THE WORLD YOU'LL LIVE IN
WILL BE <u>FILLED</u> WITH CHINESE AND KENNEDYS"

"GET IT YOURSELF
—I'M A REPUBLICAN!"

"MR. KHRUSHCHEV SAID HE LIKED YOUR STYLE IN THE STEEL CRISIS"

"—ASK WHAT YOU CAN DO FOR UNBORN GENERATIONS"

IN THE DEBRIS — HOPE?

HIS TRUTH IS MARCHING ON

"GIVE ME YOUR TIRED, YOUR POOR, YOUR BUSINESSMEN, YOUR UNIONS, YOUR...."

A NEW HOT LINE FROM THE WHITE HOUSE — TO CAPITOL HILL

"I'M UP, WORLD — READY OR NOT!"

"YOU'RE NOT LOSING A DAUGHTER
— YOU'RE GAINING A VOTE"

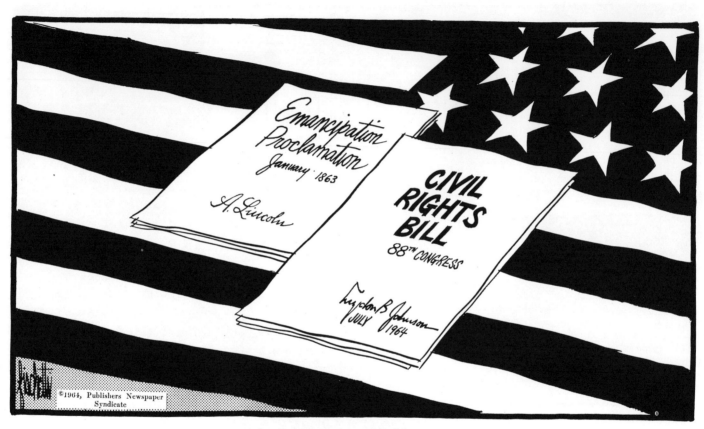

CONCEIVED IN LIBERTY

"YOU CERTAINLY HAVE TO GIVE LADY BIRD
CREDIT FOR GETTING THINGS DONE"

" —— REGRET TO INFORM YOU THAT YOUR
IMAGE WAS SEVERELY WOUNDED IN VIETNAM "

"IT JUST OCCURRED TO ME THAT YOU'RE THE ONLY
ONE IN WASHINGTON WHO'S SMILING THESE DAYS"

"BETWEEN THE CROSSES, ROW ON ROW..."

LBJ'S VERY LARGE BOOTS

"I DON'T LIKE ANY OF 'EM — MATTER OF FACT, I DON'T EVEN LIKE THE MEMBERS OF THE HATE GROUP I BELONG TO"

"IT'S THE ONLY HOUSE HAUNTED BY A LIVE MAN"

"MY CONSTITUENTS NOT ONLY DISAGREED WITH WHAT I
SAID BUT THEY TOOK ISSUE WITH MY RIGHT TO SAY IT"

"WE WENT BROKE PAYING FOR THOSE TV SPOTS AND NOW THE POLLS SHOW THAT PEOPLE THINK YOU LOOK SHIFTY"

"FRANKLY, I DON'T CARE ONE WAY OR THE OTHER ABOUT VOTER APATHY"

© 1969 Chicago Daily News

GOLDWATER'S VIETNAM CURE-ALL

STILL TRYING TO GET THAT OL' CRATE OFF THE GROUND

"IT'S THE LITTLE OLD LADIES IN SNEAKERS — THEY
WANT TO KNOW WHEN WE'RE GOING TO UNLEASH THEM"

"YOU MADE THE PANTS TOO LONG"

"I DIDN'T KNOW I WAS AN ARTIST EITHER, UNTIL PEOPLE STARTED BUYING MY STUFF"

"I CAN'T BELIEVE HE ATE THE WHOLE THING"

"WE THINK McGOVERN'S A DOG"

THE FINE PRINT

©1972 Chicago Daily News

"JUST BLOW IN MY EAR AND I'LL FOLLOW YOU ANYWHERE"

"HERE'S THE SENATOR'S SPEECH, ENID — SCRIBBLE IT
OUT IN TRIPLICATE ON THE BACKS OF ENVELOPES"

LAST LEG OF THE GREAT RACE TO MIAMI

"NED, DON'T YOU THINK WE'RE GETTING A LITTLE OLD TO BE DEMOCRATS?"

"WE'RE WAY BEHIND SCHEDULE WITH THE ARK — HOW ABOUT A RAFT?"

"I'M DELIGHTED, DICK. HOW'S THAT BUTTON
READ AGAIN — NIXON FOR WHAT?"

"IF I DIDN'T SEE IT WITH MY OWN EYES, I WOULDN'T BELIEVE IT"

"DON'T TELL THEM TO WORK WITHIN THE SYSTEM
—LOOK AT WHAT HAPPENED TO THE DEMOCRATS"

"ONLY FOUR MORE YEARS, ONLY FOUR MORE YEARS"

"HE CONSIDERS JUST GETTING TO AND FROM CONGRESS A PRODUCTIVE DAY"

"GOD'S HOUSE? NONSENSE! WE PAID FOR IT"

"WE WOULDN'T *THINK* OF USING DOGS
AGAINST NEGROES UP NORTH!"

'DEAR SON — I'M PROUD THAT YOU'RE DEFENDING
THE FREEDOM WE'RE TRYING TO GET...'

"WHAT'S DIFFERENT? WHY, IN THAT ONE, WHITEY DID HIS THING, AND IN THIS ONE, WE DO OUR THING"

"THE GOOD NEWS, I'M IN THE VANGUARD OF THE FIGHT
AGAINST INFLATION—THE BAD NEWS IS, I'M FIRED"

MEAGER GOV'T AID FOR AGED

©1971 Chicago Daily News

"I GUESS EVERYBODY'D BE HAPPIER IF OUR DAYS DWINDLED DOWN TO A PRECIOUS FEWER"

"THERE SURE IS A LOTTA YO HO HO AND DAMNED LITTLE RUM ON THIS TUB"

"I HATE TO BREAK THE NEWS TO YOU IN THE MIDDLE OF THIS GREAT SERIES ON UNEMPLOYMENT, JACK, BUT YOU'VE BEEN LAID OFF"

"IF I GIVE YOU A RAISE, I HAVE TO PASS IT ON TO THE CONSUMER, BUSINESS FALLS OFF, I HAVE TO FIRE YOU, AN' THE NEX' THING I KNOW, YOU'RE BUGGIN ME FOR A JOB"

"YOU WANTA BUST OUT?!! D'YOU KNOW WHAT IT COSTS TO LIVE LIKE THIS OUTSIDE?"

©1970 Chicago Daily News

"WHY CAN'T YOU TALK ABOUT WATERGATE LIKE EVERYBODY ELSE INSTEAD OF ALWAYS BLEATING ABOUT A RAISE?"

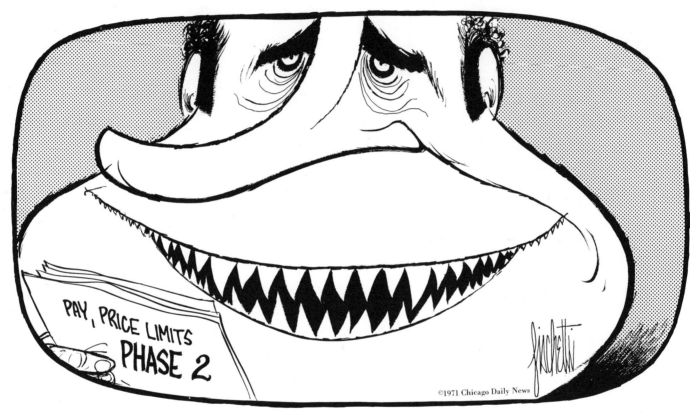

"HI, THERE..."

© 1973 Chicago Daily News

"OK, WE'LL WEAR THE TUTUS — BUT WE AIN'T GONNA DO NONE A' THAT TIPPY TOE STUFF"

THERE GOES THE NEIGHBORHOOD

"LET'S HEAR IT FOR THE LAND OF OPPORTUNITY"

"THE COUNTRY'S GOING TO THE DOGS — HAPPILY, IT'S THE TOP DOGS"

"I'M NOT WILD ABOUT NIXON BUT HE COMES CLOSEST TO MY POLITICAL PHILOSOPHY OF WHAT'S GOOD FOR ME IS GOOD FOR THE COUNTRY"

"CAREFUL, BEFORE YOU SOUND OFF ABOUT THE BRASS
—THEY'VE GOT THE EAGLE ON MY CAP BUGGED"

"I THINK IT'S ONLY FAIR TO WARN YOU THAT JOHN WAYNE'S A FRIEND OF MINE"

"IT'S THE ONLY REVENUE SHARING PLAN THAT REALLY WORKS"

©1971 Chicago Daily News

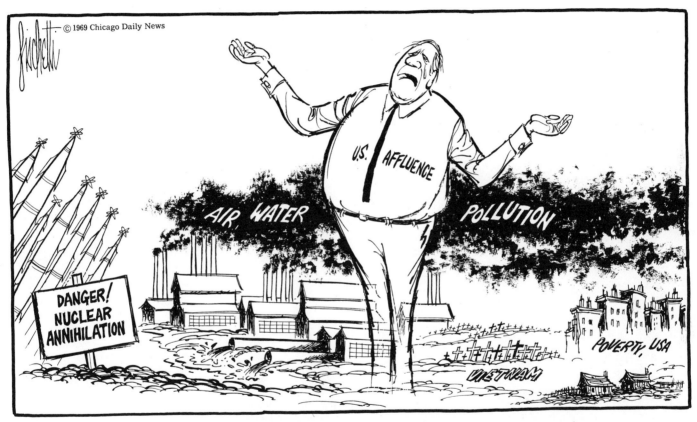

"I CAN'T UNDERSTAND KIDS TODAY — WE GAVE THEM EVERYTHING"

"—WE FIND THAT THE STUDENTS DID ATTACK NATIONAL GUARD BULLETS WITH THEIR BODIES..."

"HERE'S A GOOD SHOT OF THEIR RINGLEADER"

"YOU'RE MISSING THE _WHOLE_ POINT OF COPPING
OUT BY WANTING TO BE THE TOP COP-OUT"

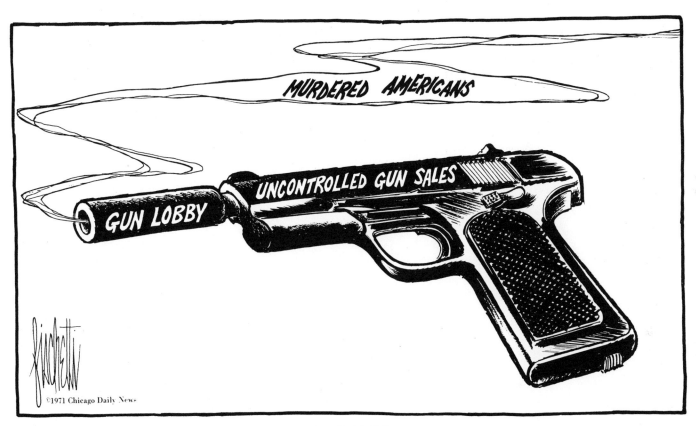

SILENCER

©1971 Chicago Daily News

"STRANGE, I WASN'T ANYWHERE NEAR ATTICA PRISON"

1970 Chicago Daily News

ROUTINE DUTY

"I DO WISH YOU'D PHONE WHEN YOU'RE
BRINGING THE JUNTA HOME FOR DINNER"

"I'M GETTING FED UP WITH THIS MIDDLE EAST TURMOIL"

"GOING AHEAD WITH OUR PLAN TO ANNIHILATE ISRAEL COULD
BRING US INTO THE TWENTIETH CENTURY IN ONE HELLUVA HURRY"

"WE'RE *VERY* CONCERNED ABOUT YOU — WE'RE DISCUSSING THE KIND OF WORLD YOU'LL BE STARVING IN"

SLAUGHTERED IRISH

©1972 Chicago Daily News

"IN THE NAME OF THE FATHER, THE SON, THE HOLY SPIRIT...AND STUPIDITY"

"THE SUN'S READY TO RISE ANY TIME YOU ARE, SIR"

"IF YOU HADN'T RESTED ON THE SEVENTH
DAY, I WOULDN'T HAVE TO WORK SO HARD"

"GET THE PROPAGANDA CHIEF DOWN HERE. I WANT HIM
TO SEE THE KIND OF LIVELY COPY I HAD IN MIND"

"HE'S ALIENATED NATIONS I'VE NEVER EVEN HEARD OF"

HISTORIC CHAPTER OR FOOTNOTE?

© 1962, New York Herald Tribune Inc.

"YOU CAN'T BEAT A FRATERNAL EMBRACE FOR GETTING CLOSE TO THE THROAT"

"HE WAS ANGRY ABOUT THE FARM MESS, STARTED BANGING HIS SHOE ON THE DESK, THE SHOE FELL APART AND <u>THEN</u> YOU SHOULD'VE HEARD HIM RANT ABOUT SHODDY CONSUMER PRODUCTS...."

"THE GOOD NEWS IS, YOUR MANUSCRIPT IS OF NOBEL PRIZE
WINNING CALIBER, THE BAD NEWS IS, YOU'RE UNDER ARREST"

"IF THERE <u>IS</u> LIFE ON VENUS
I HOPE IT DOESN'T EAT WHEAT"

"THAT'S A RELIEF — IT'S TICKING ON HIS SIDE"

" 1950, '51, '52, '53 ...... '68, '69, '70, '71 ... "

"LUCKILY, I HAVE JUST THE QUOTE FOR THIS SITUATION,
'DAMN THE TORPEDOES — FULL SPEED AHEAD!'"

"HERE'S A ROUGH ESTIMATE OF WHAT IT COSTS US TO DESTROY A BAMBOO BRIDGE IN NORTH VIETNAM—GIVE OR TAKE A MILLION"

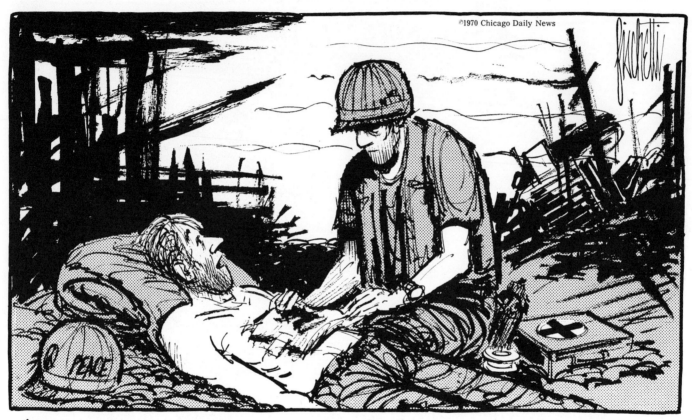

©1970 Chicago Daily News

"HEALTHY MEN HAVE BEEN THE CURSE OF MY FAMILY LINE — WE ALL WIND UP DEAD SOLDIERS"

"Y'CAN'T GET BETTER TRAININ' THAN THIS FOR BEIN' AN UNEMPLOYED CIVILIAN"

WHEN THE SAINTS COME MARCHING IN

"WE'VE BEEN DECLASSIFIED"

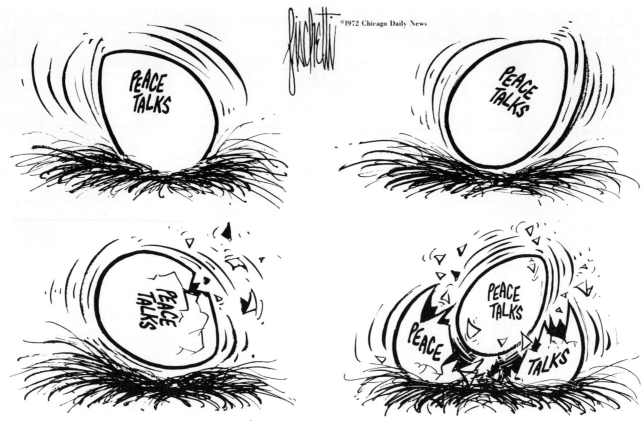

THE HATCHING

THIEU'S GAME PLAN

©1972 Chicago Daily News

'PEACE IS AT HAND'

DR. STRANGEDOVE

PEACE IS AT HAND

©1972 Chicago Daily News

VIETNAM
PEACE
ACCORD

Thank God!
Hanoi
U.S.A.

INITIALED

THE UNKNOWN SOLDIER

"DEAR PRESIDENT NIXON... WHAT REALLY TICKLED MY FUNNY BONE WAS WHEN
YOU SAID YOU WERE SENDING TROOPS TO CAMBODIA TO SAVE LIVES..."

"YOU'RE BETTER PREPARED TO BE PRESIDENT THAN I WAS
—THEY'VE ALREADY CALLED YOU EVERYTHING IN THE BOOK"

"IT'S BEEN NINE MONTHS AND HE'S <u>STILL</u> NOT SUITED UP"

"THIS PLAY IS VERY, VERY COMPLICATED — EVEN I DON'T UNDERSTAND IT, AND I CREATED IT"

©1971 Chicago Daily News

"WATCH YOUR LANGUAGE, FELLA — DO YOU KNOW WHO YOU'RE TALKING TO?... I'M A FRIEND OF JOHN CONNALLY"

JOHN WAYNE VIEW OF 'PETTY' WATERGATE ISSUE

TRUE GRIT

© 1973 Chicago Daily News

ADMINISTRATION STRONG MAN

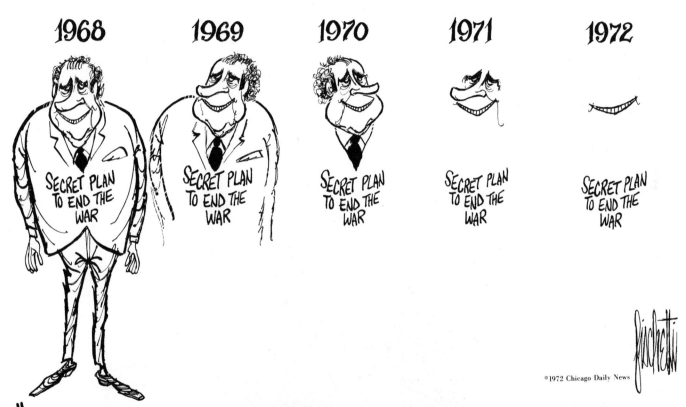

"— IT VANISHED QUITE SLOWLY... AND ENDING WITH THE GRIN, WHICH REMAINED SOME TIME AFTER THE REST OF IT HAD GONE..." — THE CHESHIRE CAT IN ALICE IN WONDERLAND

"... HALT THE EROSION OF MORAL FIBER IN AMERICAN LIFE AND THE DENIAL OF INDIVIDUAL ACCOUNTABILITY FOR INDIVIDUAL ACTION" — PRESIDENT NIXON

"SO MUCH FOR REPUBLICAN FINGERPRINTS ALL OVER THE PLACE—NOW LET'S LOOK FOR CLUES"

CREDIBILITY

WATERGATE TESTIMONY

THE SHREDDER

©1973 Chicago Daily News

"—IT HAS COME TO MY ATTENTION..."

THE LAW-AND-ORDER ADMINISTRATION TEAM PLAYERS

"GEE WHILLIKERS, I SAID WHEN I FOUND OUT WHAT MY STAFF WAS UP TO"

© 1973 Chicago Daily News

"GOD BLESS AMERICA AND GOD BLESS EACH AND EVERY ONE OF YOU EXCEPT JOHN DEAN"

"I'M PERFECTLY CONTENT NOT TO HAVE A LIGHT AT THE END OF MY TUNNEL"

© 1973 Chicago Daily News

—THE PRESIDENT HAS INHERENT POWER TO AUTHORIZE BURGLARIES WHENEVER NECESSARY...
—EHRLICHMAN

MINE EYES HAVE SEEN THE GLORY OF...

THE NIXON LIBRARY

THE LIGHT AT THE END OF THE WATERGATE TUNNEL